ART
imitating
LIFE
imitating
DEATH

IRISHTOWN PRESS

ART imitating LIFE imitating DEATH

An exploration of *Guests of the Nation*
by Frank O'Connor

Cónal Creedon

IRISHTOWN PRESS

Awarded The Gold Award for
European Non-Fiction at
IP Book Awards USA 2023.

Awarded The Silver Award for
International Reference at
IP Book Awards USA 2023.

The Independent Publisher Book Awards is a program established in the United
States to honour exemplary books.

Reviews

Highlights of 2022 – Cónal Creedon chronicler supreme of Cork city life – *Art Imitating Life, Imitating Death*, coinciding with the centenary commemoration.
Marjorie Brennan –THE IRISH EXAMINER

Books of Year 2022. – In Cork, we are blessed with such an array of literary talent that we can not only shop local, but read local. In Art Imitating Life Imitating Death, Cónal Creedon delves deep into the origins of Guests Of The Nation by fellow Cork writer Frank O'Connor.
Grainne McGuinness – THE ECHO LIVE

The Best Book Produced – would be Cónal Creedon's, *Art Imitating Life, imitating Death*, in his exploration of Guests Of The Nation by Frank O'Connor. And there is so much to explore. I was particularly taken by Creedon's research into the character Noble, one of the IRA men holding the two British soldiers. [Creedon] deeply embodied with his own knowledge of the place – gave him extra emotional connection to the story.
Declan Lynch – THE SUNDAY INDEPENDENT

Cónal Creedon's contributions to Ireland's and international arts and letters are legion and nearly legendary among his fans. This volume publishes his original lecture exploring the memorable short story "Guests of the Nation" by eminent Irish author Frank O'Connor.

In 2003, Creedon was commissioned by the Irish National Broadcaster, RTÉ, to adapt "Guests of the Nation" as a radio play as part of the centenary celebrations of Frank O'Connor's birth. "And so," he says, "I set about deconstructing the story and exploring O'Connor's work from the perspective of a writer rather than a reader… a more intense level of focus."

It is likely not an overstatement or hyperbole to suggest that Creedon understands this story better than most writers and readers worldwide. It also seems not coincidental that both O'Connor and Creedon were/are Cork natives. Creedon's examination of O'Connor's text is steeped in both men's literary talents and their understanding of what transpired in Irish history to motivate the writing of and the consequential interest in this story. Creedon's thorough analysis of the story's significance touches on several points in brief but comprehensive chapters.

Creedon succinctly explores details about this retributive execution and related historical events in which strong bonds of friendship arise between sworn enemies, with the most logical conclusion that the capture and execution of Compton-Smith have the greatest number of similarities to the "Guests of the Nation" plot. The brief but thorough and fascinating analysis is followed by Creedon's radio script, an adaptation of O'Connor's original story. Creedon is well-known for the quality and depth of his sixty-plus hours of original radio dramas.

The third part of this volume is an extended, online Covid-era conversation between the author and Dr. Conci Mazzullo (University of Catania). The text explores many questions that Creedon fans would ask about his family life in Cork City that led to his devotion to the arts and literature and the many historical changes across Ireland and N. Ireland that have influenced his body of published work. As such, this book is a compelling biographical piece that touches upon so many facets of Creedon's life and letters that readers will hope for a much larger and more comprehensive biography or memoir soon. This volume is a significant guide not only to the O'Connor story he examines but also to some important facets of Ireland's national history that drive Creedon's motivations as a writer.

RECOMMENDED by the US Review

Kate Robinson – US REVIEW OF BOOKS

The scintillating tale is once again recaptured in [Creedon's] new book, Art imitating Life imitating Death.

Cónal's meticulous research also unpicked another interesting thread to the story. Art imitating Life imitating Death gives the reader an insight into the mind of one fascinating Cork writer, Creedon, contemplating another, resulting in the fleshing out of O'Connor's story, and adding a further layer of understanding into the fabric of some of the most emotionally elevated and traumatically charged days of Ireland's troubled past.

Cónal's memory is redolent with scenes of the colourful life all around him growing up in a busy shop in Cork city, and as Irish society went through ever increasing changes towards a more secular society, Cónal experienced it all through the lens of his teenage years and into young adulthood.

Aisling Meath – THE EVENING ECHO

In this fascinating book, Cónal Creedon gives some more details about Major Geoffrey Lee Compton-Smith who died nobly and fearlessly. His wife had believed he was abducted off-duty, out for a stroll, but the major was not aware that it was revealed in a House of Commons statement that he had had a tryst with a nurse in Blarney when he was captured.

In 2003, RTÉ commissioned the Cork-born writer and documentary filmmaker Cónal Creedon to adapt O'Connor's short story as a radio play, the text of which is included in this book. If you are familiar with the original format it is fascinating to see how the text of the radio play has been sublimated and transformed, drawing us intimately into the moral dilemma facing the callow IRA protagonists who have now been ordered to shoot and bury the two soldiers with whom they have become friends.

Creedon was familiar with the short story collection Guests of the Nation from his school syllabus but in Art imitating Life imitating Death he does us the favour of exploring in detail the real story of Compton-Smith. The book also contains a fascinating interview with Creedon from, *Studi irlandesi: A Journal of Irish Studies* reprising his writing career, dedication to the arts and analyses of some of his novels, including the quite brilliant, multi-layered, funny and touching Begotten Not Made.

Danny Morrison – THE IRISH EXAMINER

It was such a gripping event Cónal Creedon could have filled 2 hours, never mind one, and we'd still have hung on every word. Stories linking stories, and fact at times more fascinating than fiction. Well, both of us left, all fired up to do more reading about Lucas! I actually didn't know any of that. It was brilliant.

Elmarie Mawe – THE ARTS SHOW 96FM

In his telling of these stories, Cónal took many tangents weaving a fascinating spider's web of intrigue and mystery which shines a light on an aspect of our history which has been mostly hidden or, at least unexplored. This makes the book a treasure.

Concubhar Ó Liatháin – INDEPENDENT.IE

4th Battalion IRA, photographed on 19th February 1921.

The following day, 20th February, at an isolated safe house in Clonmult, County Cork, twelve volunteers of 4th Battalion, IRA were shot dead. Two volunteers were taken into custody, court-martialled and sentenced to death. On 23rd March, at Ballycannon, on the northside of Cork City, six volunteers found sleeping in a safe house barn were shot dead by crown forces. On 28th April 1921, Maurice Moore and Patrick O'Sullivan (IRA volunteers captured at Clonmult) and Tomas Mulcahy and Patrick Ronayne (IRA volunteers captured at Mourneabbey) were executed at Victoria Barracks, Cork.

Two days later, on 30th April, in response to the executions, Major Geoffrey Lee Compton-Smith was executed in Donoughmore, County Cork by the IRA.

Dedication

When old schoolmates meet the conversations invariably come around to those significant educators who offered inspiration and guidance during the all-important formative years.

I wish to dedicate this book to Ms Marie Collins, my 1st Class teacher at Eason's Hill School, Brother Dáithí O Connell, my 6th Class teacher at the North Monastery Primary School, Cork and to Mr. Humphrey Twomey, my Intermediate Certificate, History and English teacher. Three educators who instinctively understood the importance of *mol an óige* and stretched the parameters of education far beyond the limitations of an academic syllabus.

Published in 2022 by Irishtown Press

irishtownpress@gmail.com

The moral right of the author has been asserted.

A catalogue record for this book is available from the British Library.

ISBN 978-1-7399180-6-4 (paperback)

ISBN 978-1-7399180-7-1 (hardcover)

Contents

Foreword

When the Swiss Centre of Irish Studies was founded in 2019, one of its initial aims was to organize a series of events to commemorate the centenary of the Irish revolutionary period. The first of these was to be a small meet-and-greet type symposium, where Swiss scholars working in fields related to Irish Studies would come together and get to know one another while listening to a series of lectures from invited speakers. From the beginning, we wanted to stress the inter-disciplinary nature of our newly established Centre and so we set about creating a programme that would feature historians, literary scholars, filmmakers and writers. In Cónal Creedon, we found some-one with the rare ability to fit into all of the aforementioned categories. Not only is he at home in a variety of disciplines, but so much of his work is connected to the revolutionary period, be it his televi-sion documentaries *The Burning of Cork* (2005) and *Why the Guns Remained Silent in Rebel Cork* (2006), his history book *The Immortal Deed of Michael O'Leary* (2015), or his radio play adaptation of Frank O'Connor's short story "Guests of the Nation" (2003). It was the last of these works that particularly piqued our interest, especially when we learned of the many real-world parallels he'd discovered when doing research for the adaptation.

And so it was that, on 24th January 2020, Cónal drew our inaugu-ral symposium to a close with his lecture "Art Imitating Life Imitating Death". An exploration of "Guests of the Nation" by Frank O'Connor, followed by a wonderful presentation of the original RTÉ produc-tion of his radio play. The lecture took the audience on a journey down the backroads and boreens of rural Cork during the War of Independence, recounting how the IRA moved its prisoners from safe house to safe house, and how, as in O'Connor's famous story, the amount of time that captors and captives spent at close quarters sometimes led to the unlikeliest of friendships. To illustrate that point, Cónal presented us with a couple of fascinating accounts of surprisingly warm Anglo-Irish relations during that otherwise violent period. The first involved the IRA's well-publicised kidnapping of a high-ranking British officer, Brigadier-General Cuthbert Lucas, whom they treated to fishing expeditions, bottles of whiskey and nightly poker games before ultimately releasing him unharmed. The second was the similarly high-profile kidnapping of a British officer, Major Geoffrey Lee Compton-Smith, who, likewise, was treated kindly by his captors, but who went on to meet a much more tragic end, one not unlike that of Belcher and Hawkins in "Guests of the Nation".

"Guests of the Nation," for those who may be unfamiliar with it, is one of the most famous Irish short stories and one which has left a significant imprint on Irish culture more generally. It has been adapted for both stage and screen and was also the inspiration behind Brendan Behan's play *The Hostage* and Neil Jordan's Academy Award-winning film *The Crying Game*. At its core, it is the story of Bonaparte and Noble, two IRA volunteers, who befriend Belcher and Hawkins, the two English soldiers they are holding as prisoners, only to be ordered to execute them at the end of the narrative. The story is told from the perspective of Bonaparte, who looks back on this killing as the moment that changed his life forever, leading to one of the most memorable closing lines in Irish literature: "And anything that happened me afterwards, I never felt the same about again."

The success or failure of any adaptation of this story invariably hinges upon how well the writer can make the audience feel for the characters involved. The greater the warmth of the relationship between the IRA and their "guests", the greater the moral dilemma when Jeremiah Donovan finally shows up with the order for them to execute the prisoners. In this regard, Cónal's radio play is a resounding success. He presents his audience with well-rounded characters, whose affection for one another is eminently palpable. This is especially true of Belcher and the woman of the house, whose tender early-morning exchanges before the rest of the household has woken up contribute greatly to the pathos at the climax of the play. The same applies to the relationship between Hawkins and Noble. In the hands of a lesser writer, their constant arguments could come across as annoying, but Cónal's wonderful ear for dialogue, coupled with his signature humour, elevates their discussions from simple bickering to good-natured banter. The scenes around the card table, in particular, are great fun, revealing how comfortable the characters all are in one another's company, with even the woman of the house joining in the gentle teasing. It is this easy sense of camaraderie that serves to make Jeremiah's shock announcement all the more devastating for those involved – and indeed for the audience.

Sitting in the half-light of the darkened auditorium on that January evening in Zurich, watching the audience be transported through time and space to a bog in County Cork a century ago, I was struck by how vital and fresh O'Connor's story still is, and how, in the hands of a gifted playwright like Cónal Creedon, it packs a powerful punch. What is more, familiarity with the text doesn't necessarily prepare the audience for the impact of the ending. Even though you know the execution is coming, you can't help but hope against all hope – like Hawkins – that friendship will win out over duty and that the prisoners' lives will ultimately be spared. When that doesn't happen, what remains is an emptiness and a feeling of senselessness that is hard to shake. And so, like Bonaparte, the audience find themselves transformed by the experience. This is the power of great literature, courtesy of two of Cork's finest.

Dr Shane Walshe

The Swiss Centre of Irish Studies
The Zurich James Joyce Foundation
English Department
University of Zurich
Switzerland

Before I Begin

In January 2020, I was invited by the Swiss Centre of Irish Studies at the University of Zurich and the Zurich James Joyce Foundation to present a lecture at a symposium (Title: From Independence to Civil War: The Irish Revolutionary Period).

The symposium in Zurich, a city synonymous with one of Cork's greatest literary grandsons, James Joyce – offered me the opportunity to revisit and contextualise a theory I had first put forward in 2016 (The Holly Bough 2016), in which I explored the links between the fiction of Frank O'Connor's Guests of the Nation and the factual killing of Major Geoffrey Lee Compton-Smith by the IRA in mid-Cork.

The symposium was an overwhelming success, delegates received such a wonderful welcome, and the social gatherings offered a powerful opportunity to integrate with new people and engage with new thoughts and ideas.

Zurich is a fascinating city, I vowed to return during Summer 2020. Alas, I could not have anticipated that within weeks, the world as we knew it would stop spinning, struck by a global catastrophe of biblical proportion, and life would enter an interminable and unprecedented phase of lockdowns compounded by mandatory social isolation.

I am very grateful to Michael C. Frank, Frances Ilmberger, Anne-Claire Michoux, Martin Mühlheim and Shane Walshe of the English Department in Zurich University, and Ruth Frehner, Silke Stebler, Fritz Senn and Ursula Zeller of the James Joyce Foundation Zurich, for inviting me to participate in the symposium – memories of those enlightening and engaging days in Zurich stood me in good stead during the ensuing repressive restrictions of Covid-tide.

In March 2021, the lecture I presented at Zurich University (Title: Art Imitating Life Imitating Death) was published by *Studi irlandesi. A Journal of Irish Studies* at the University of Florence. The opportunity to engage with Fiorenzo Fantaccini, general editor of the Journal, Arianna Antonielli and Samuele Grassi, respectively

Journal Manager and Review Editor of *Studi irlandesi* <https://oajournals.fupress.net/index.php/bsfm-sijis/index> – was such an uplifting experience during the darkest days of the pandemic. It gave purpose to what would have otherwise been an extremely rudderless time. And, of course, I always treasure the opportunity to work with Fiorenzo Fantaccini – we first met back in 2001 when he translated my novel, *Passion Play*. Translation of my work is a most special privilege, and such a wonderful introduction to Italy. Thank you, Fiorenzo, my friend. And thanks to Firenze Unversity Press (FUP) for granting permission to reprint my essay "Art Imitating Life Imitating Death. An exploration of 'Guests of the Nation' by Frank O'Connor", published in *Studi irlandesi. A Journal of Irish Studies*, 11 (2011), pp. 271 – 297, and the interview "The Joy of Writing after 20 years. In conversation with Cónal Creedon", conducted by Conci Mazzullo, and published in *Studi irlandesi. A Journal of Irish Studies*, 10 (2020), pp. 253 – 295.

Special thanks also to Conci Mazzullo for inviting me to engage in the extensive interview included in this publication, originally published in *Studi irlandesi. A Journal of Irish Studies* in 2020. Conci Mazzullo is a diamond, and despite the frustrations and hurdles of social and geographic distance, compounded by the technological gymnastics required to conduct such a protracted project during Covid-tide – Conci's tenacity and focus overcame all adversity and challenges. Grazie assai, Conci.

I wish to extend my heartfelt gratitude to all of you for your commitment, encouragement and patience.

It takes a city to bring a manuscript from page to bookshop shelf. I am very grateful to John Foley and Lisa Sheridan of Bite Design – who have been integral and instrumental in the bringing together of this publication. I would like to add my special appreciation to those who have been a constant source of support to my endeavours. I am blessed with so many friends, family and neighbours who continue to offer me unconditional encouragement, far too many to mention you all here by name.

And of course, to Fiona O'Toole with love: fearless in the face of adversity, calm in the eye of a storm and always such a fun person to be with.

Frank O'Connor.

LECTURE: Art Imitating Life Imitating Death. An exploration of Guests of the Nation by Frank O'Connor was first presented as a lecture by Cónal Creedon at the Swiss Centre of Irish Studies at the University of Zurich and the Zurich James Joyce Foundation on 24th January 2020.

PUBLICATION: Art Imitating Life Imitating Death. An exploration of Guests of the Nation by Frank O'Connor was first published in *Studi irlandesi. A Journal of Irish Studies*. https://oajournals.fupress.net/index.php/bsfm-sijis A Journal of Irish Studies, Firenze University Press, Italy, 2021.

ABSTRACT: In 2003, as part of the centenary celebrations for Frank O'Connor's birth, I was commissioned by the Irish National Broadcaster [RTÉ] to adapt O'Connor's short story *Guests of the Nation* for radio. My research led me to a number of real-life incidents that echoed O'Connor's emotionally charged exploration of the tragic consequences when friendships are formed between sworn enemies in a time of war. In the twilight zone where life imitates art, in 2012, I was invited by descendants of the IRA Unit who had kidnapped and executed Major Compton-Smith, to visit the isolated farmhouse in which he had been held hostage. I welcome you to join me on my journey into a world where history and story go hand in hand, and fact and fiction dovetail together seamlessly without contradiction or contrivance.

KEYWORDS: Fiction, Frank O'Connor, Irish War of Independence, Short Story, Hostage, History.

OPEN ACCESS

CITATION: C. Creedon (2021) Art Imitating Life Imitating Death. An exploration of "Guests of the Nation" by Frank O'Connor. Sijis 11: pp. 271-297. ISSN 2239-3978 (online) doi: 10.13128/SIJIS-2239-3978-12888

DATA AVAILABILITY STATEMENT: All relevant data are within the paper and its Supporting Information files.

COMPETING INTERESTS: The Author(s) declare(s) no conflict of interest.

Art Imitating Life Imitating Death.

An exploration of *Guests of the Nation*
by Frank O'Connor

Cónal Creedon
Adjunct Professor of Creative Writing,
School of English, UCC
irishtownpress@gmail.com

Frank O'Connor creates a colourful and textured narrative that captures the Cork City of my childhood in all its idiosyncrasy and eccentricity. Born on Douglas Street and reared in Harrington's Square [via Blarney Street], O'Connor was a neighbour's child. He was one of our own. His words were our words. His stories were our stories. His characters were steeped in our parish yet resonated across the planet. Embraced by Irish-America at a time when the recently established Republic of Ireland was taking its first faltering steps as an independent nation, O'Connor cast a larger-than-life shadow from the footlights of the world stage. Meanwhile, here in his home-town, we basked in the reflected glow of his global glory.

I first came upon *Guests of the Nation* in the pages of *Exploring English I*, my Intermediate Certificate school anthology (MARTIN 2011 [1967])[1]. Barely a teenager, I was bored by textbook experts spouting

---

1   Great credit is due to Augustine Martin, the editor of this anthology of short stories. This collection of short fiction originally intended as a school textbook in the mid-1960s became so popular that it was republished "by public demand" forty-five years after it was first published and became a bestseller.

textbook theories. The education I craved was to be found beyond the school gates, for out there was the greatest educator of all – life itself. My rampant imagination ran with the fox and chased with the hound. But then, one day, while thumbing through my schoolbook, my fingers hesitated at *Guests of the Nation*. Something about that story just stopped me in my tracks. Seduced by a narrative that was deeply rooted in a culture, a history and a landscape so familiar to me, I was captivated by this wartime parable, that somehow elevated me above the tedium of the classroom. In time, O'Connor's curly tales of shawlies, (MARTIN 2017)[2] steps and steeples, became like a gateway drug that unlocked the magical mystical world of Irish literature in the mind of this adventure-seeking youth.

In retrospect, I now understand why *Guests of the Nation* made such a profound impression on me at that time. I was twelve years of age, and Ireland was a place of rapid change just as I was coming of age. The cosy cartel of church and state that had been enshrined and embraced since the formation of the Irish Free State[3] was beginning to show hairline cracks, and after eight hundred years of asset stripping and despotism as a colony of our nearest neighbour, the Republic of Ireland was finally getting up off its knees and finding its "place among the nations of the earth" (VANCE 1982, 185)[4]. The island of Ireland was in transition – a short few decades had passed since independence, and the capital 'R' of Revisionism was poking its finger in and around the soft underbelly of Irish sacred cows (COSTELLO 2014).

Something momentous happened in 1970, when a young Catholic schoolgirl stepped out from behind the sectarian barricades of Derry

---

2   Shawlies – a name given to a very specific class of Cork women of an earlier generation, identified by the distinctive black shawl they wore. Usually working-class women, fruit sellers, street vendors – renowned for their sharp wit and cutting turn of phrase.
3   The Irish Free State was established in 1922 in the aftermath of the Irish War of Independence.
4   This is a reference to "Robert Emmet's Speech from the Dock", in which, the Irish patriot Robert Emmet, facing execution after the failed rebellion of 1803, insists that his epitaph should not be written, and no headstone should be erected in his honour until Ireland is free and independent and "takes its place among the nations of the earth".

(LONDONDERRY; FERGUSON 2015)[5] in Northern Ireland (The North of Ireland) and won the Eurovision Song Contest for the Republic of Ireland. Her gentle song of love soared above the sabre rattling, gunfire, rioting and unrest. And when the British tabloids asked what sort of a name Dana was, they were told it was an Irish name meaning bold, fearless, or brave. Just as the word *Derry* was an Irish word for oak wood, and the very notion of coupling it with the word *London* was but a farcical statement of dominion.

Down south of the border, the lines of demarcation between Catholic, Republican and Nationalist had become so tangled, entwined, and confused, that when Dana and her mother were invited by the Catholic Bishop of Derry to receive a blessing before setting out for Europe, it left us in no doubt, but that Dana was singing for Ireland; a holy Catholic and united Ireland (SCALLON 1999, 13).

It is difficult to contextualise or quantify the significance of Ireland winning the Eurovision Song Contest in 1970. When Dana appeared on every single television screen across the land, live from Amsterdam in her white *bánín* dress embellished with ancient Celtic knots of emerald green, it was as if a united Ireland had stepped onto the world stage wrapped in the tricolour of the Republic. There was something about those seemingly inconsequential three minutes of popular music history that fed into the lifeblood, soul and marrow of the nation – it was as if, for the first time since partition, Ireland, north and south of the border, was united as one.

---

5   Derry or Londonderry? What's in a name? The London prefix was added to Derry when the city was granted a Royal Charter by King James I in 1613. The name, Derry, with its connection to the ancient Gaelic name of the city is preferred by nationalists and it is broadly used throughout Northern Ireland's Nationalist community. For the most part, Derry is also used south of the border in the Republic of Ireland. Unionists prefer the name Londonderry. However, I am reliably informed that Derry is also used by most residents of the city – Nationalist & Unionist.

There exists a similar cultural and political schism regarding the name of a relatively small north-eastern portion of the Island of Ireland. Ever since the The Government of Ireland Act 1920 & Anglo-Irish Treaty 1922, this specific six counties which is part of the nine counties that make up the Irish province of Ulster is known variously as The North of Ireland or Northern Ireland? Ulster or the six counties? Depending on which side of the political or cultural divide one is aligned.

At that time, Ireland was seldom represented on the world stage, so, to witness Dana standing toe to toe against all comers and emerge victorious, imbued a spiralling sense of national pride. Dana highlighted the notion that nationalist Ireland was one nation divided by a man-made line drawn on a map – and the ink was still wet. For my generation, it seemed to mark the moment when everything changed. Europe, which had always been such a faraway and exotic place, now seemed somehow closer,[6] and the Irish were standing proudly centre stage at the heart of it. We had taken our first tentative steps to align ourselves with the Continent on an equal footing and, in doing so, had further severed the apron strings of the toxic and unequal arrangement that had existed between Ireland and our nearest neighbour since the arrival of Strongbow back in the eleventh century.

1970s Ireland seemed politically charged and ideologically confused. The fiftieth anniversary of the Easter 1916 Rising (FOY, BARTON 2011)[7] had rekindled the flames of nationalism. The Republic was experiencing its first flush of nationhood. The martyrs of 1916, who had laid down their lives, were eulogised from every parish pump and pulpit to the point of beatification. The GPO[8] in Dublin had become our *Alamo* — a venerated shrine of national pilgrimage to hold dear the blood sacrifice of a failed rebellion.

But amid all the flag waving and cheering, several complicating loose ends of history remained untethered and dangling. Not least the glaring anomaly that the planned commemoration of the 1916 Rising happened to coincide with the fiftieth anniversary of World War One – a conflict of far greater tragedy in terms of carnage, in which almost quarter of a million Irishmen volunteered to join the British army and march through the blood-drenched fields of

6   Dana (1970), 'All Kinds Of Everything' – *Eurovision Song Contest* – Amsterdam, https://www.youtube.com/watch?v=8xmnd3uiK_Y (03/2021)
7   Ireland has a long and gory history of failed rebellions, risings and insurrections, but the failed rebellion that took place in Ireland at Easter 1916 holds a special significance and continues to be a hot topic of debate right to the present.
8   The General Post Office, O'Connell Street, Dublin. GPO was the headquarters of the Irish Rebels during the 1916 Rising.

Flanders to fight for *King and Country*. To add further complication to the national celebrations, fifty years had also passed since The Irish War of Independence (1919–1921). This exposed the convoluted irony that while many Irishmen had volunteered to fight for the British army during World War One in the blind belief that they were fighting for the *freedom of small nations* (COLLINS 2014), the British authorities had no qualms about executing the Irishmen who had attempted to free the small nation of Ireland from British rule during the 1916 Rising. When the Great War ended – like Óisín on his return from Tír na nÓg,[9] many Irishmen returned home to a dramatically changed Ireland, a people who had been militarised and politicised, a land where all had 'changed and changed utterly' (YEATS 1989, 287).[10] And so, some former British soldiers joined the survivors of the 1916 Rising in the ranks of the IRA[11] and went on to play a pivotal role in the war against Britain during the Irish War of Independence (MCGREEVY 2020A).

But then the most difficult commemoration of all – The Civil War. How would the fledgling Irish Republic mark the fiftieth anniversary of the unholy trinity of truce, treaty and civil war (KISSANE 2005). Therein lay a twisted tragedy of interconnecting events; a chaotic period of savage and personalised bloodletting between former comrades that ended in vindictive stalemate. Some might argue that the Irish Civil War never did end. The battle lines remained intact, the conflict just moved from the rural heartlands and city street corners into the newly established Irish Free State Parliament, where former comrades continued to face each other as enemies across the floor of Dáil Éireann (the lower house and principal chamber of

---

9   Óisín is a character in Irish mythology who had been away from Ireland in Tír na nÓg for a short while. On his return, Ireland had undergone such dramatic change in his absence that it was unrecognisable.

10 'changed, changed utterly: A terrible beauty is born' – is the iconic line from the poem, Easter 1916, by WB Yeats.

11 The IRA - Irish Republican Army. A paramilitary organisation, that has reinvented/regenerated itself on various occasions. It was first officially established in 1919 as a natural successor to the IRB (Irish Republican Brotherhood 1858 to 1924). The IRA (1919), The Official IRA (1969-1972), The Provisional IRA (1969), The Continuity IRA (1986), The Real IRA (1997), etc.

the Irish government), and the vitriolic war of words and ideologies continued to rage day after day.

My teenage years saw a heightened sense of nationalist fervour running rampant throughout the country. The scars of unresolved conflicts that had been festering for decades were once again rising to the surface in a weeping open wound. And while the Republic of Ireland was struggling with the contradictions of the past, a few miles up the road, the North of Ireland was focused on resolving the complications of the present. North of the border had become a powder keg set to explode. News was filtering south of civil rights denied and the persecution of Catholics. The escalating sectarianism saw northern nationalists burnt from their homes and forced to flee to the South with nothing but the shirts on their backs. British troops were once again on the streets of Ireland. Catholics were manning the barricades of Free Derry Corner, the carnage of Bloody Sunday (MCGLINCHEY 2019, 161)[12] made a shocked international media sit up and take notice (MCCANN 2006, 4). This pressure cooker of rising tension set the scene for what some would view as the generational mandatory split in the ranks of militant nationalism (TURNER 2002)[13]. The Official IRA stepped back into the shadows. Meanwhile, amid rumours of southern Irish government ministers actively gunrunning to the North (HENEY 2020), the Provisional IRA were busy replacing the *pike in the thatch* (O'TOOLE 2012)[14] with an Armalite (WHITE 1993, 81).

In keeping with the sense of militant urgency of the times, The

12 Bloody Sunday (Bogside Massacre). On 30th January 1972, British soldiers shot 26 civilians during a protest march in Derry. Fourteen people died: 13 were killed outright. The British soldiers were from the 1st Battalion, Parachute Regiment – also implicated in the Ballymurphy Massacre on 11th August 1971.
13 Renowned Irish writer, wit and IRA volunteer, Brendan Behan once described the tendency of militant republicanism to split with each new generation as – the first item on any republican agenda is the split in the organisation following the previous meeting.
14 'Pike in the Thatch' – is a metaphorical symbol of revolutionary readiness. Historically, in the aftermath of defeat, Irish rebels would hide their weapons [pikes] in the thatched roof of their cottages, to be used when the time came for the next generation of Irish revolutionaries to step forward.

Dubliners[15] were belting out *The Merry Ploughboy*[16] with its simple unambiguous message that we should all pick up a gun and join the IRA. And though the song celebrated the IRA of a previous generation, it captured the mood in the country – a new day had dawned and regardless of what shade of green was recruiting beneath the tricolour, the IRA was the IRA. The song became an extremely popular street ballad that climbed to the top of the Irish music charts within days of its release and held that position for six weeks – and every child old enough to shoulder a hurley or a hockey stick joined in the chorus.

> We're off to join the IRA.
> And we're off tomorrow morn.
> Where the bayonets clash, and the rifles flash,
> to the echo of the Thompson gun.[17]

So, when I first stumbled upon *Guests of the Nation* by Frank O'Connor in the pages of my *Exploring English I*, Intermediate Certificate anthology, my imagination was fertile ground. This tale of reprisal and counter-reprisal held up a mirror to real-life events unfolding north and south of the border, right across the island of Ireland. I felt compelled to follow O'Connor's tale on a journey to the beating heart of Irish nationalism.

Guests of the Nation is an exploration of friendships, ideologies and divided loyalties – tested against the cold brutality of duty. Set against the spiralling violence of the Irish War Of Independence, *Guests of the Nation* creates a world where history and story go hand in hand. Though often cited as a powerful anti-war story, it

---

15   The Dubliners – an Irish folk group who spearheaded the ballad singing era of the late 1960s – 1970s.

16   The Merry Ploughboy, a hit single by Dermot O'Brien and the Clubmen in 1966. It reached the top of the Irish music charts in only seven days and held that position for six weeks in late 1966. [Nielsen Business Media, Inc. (Oct 8, 1966) Nielsen Business Media, Inc. pp. 32.]

17   The Dubliners. The Merry Ploughboy. YouTube. https://www.youtube.com/watch?v=VR12Q4kcdqQ

seemed to tap into the renewed nationalism that was taking root in 1970s Ireland. Maybe that's why the crisis of conscience explored in O'Connor's tragic anti-war story seemed to justify the extreme personalised bloodletting that occurs in a time of war, particularly in the context of a guerrilla war.

The story unfolds in a small, isolated hillside cottage where two young and inexperienced IRA volunteers (Noble and Bonaparte) are set with the task of guarding two captured British soldiers (Belcher and Hawkins). In a classic example of *The Stockholm Syndrome* (WESTCOTT 2013)[18] a familiarity between captors and captives develops into a deep and profound friendship, a friendship enhanced by the maternal presence of the woman of the house. This amiable and comfortable dynamic is interrupted from time to time, when the IRA commander, Jeremiah O'Donovan, calls to the cottage to check up on his raw recruits and the hostages. But when Jeremiah O'Donovan eventually would take his leave and disappear off into the night, life in the homestead would relax and return to normal, and the camaraderie between adversaries continued to grow.

The blossoming friendship between friend and foe is typified by the constant banter between the young IRA volunteer, Noble, and the British soldier, Hawkins. They engage with each other like two young bucks, their antlers locked in eternal conflict. Meanwhile, Belcher, the older more philosophical of the two British soldiers, steps comfortably into his role of man about the house, fetching water, chopping wood, and generally making himself useful. Belcher quickly establishes a gentlemanly and caring relationship with the woman of the house. This could well be interpreted as his personal desire for the domesticity of family life, particularly in light of his revelation later in the story that his own wife and child had left him, and in civilian life he was effectively alone.

The other young IRA volunteer, Bonaparte, is the narrator of this story. He is contemplative by nature and seems more mature than

18 Stockholm Syndrome is a condition in which hostages develop a psychological bond with their captors during captivity.

Cork City Volunteers. Courtesy Cork City Museum.

his comrade Noble. As the narrator of the piece, Bonaparte seems removed from the main action. His mind internalising and analysing the unfolding situation as he struggles to make sense of the friendship that develops between sworn enemies. Bonaparte's detachment is brought into sharp focus at the end of the story when he finds himself centre stage – his finger on the trigger, the barrel of his gun pressed to Belcher's head.

The intensity of this ever-deepening bond between enemies is accentuated by the claustrophobic intimacy of the isolated setting. This is a friendship fuelled by late-night card playing and kindled with fiery discourse on such diverse topics as the merits of capitalism over socialism and the existence of God. Meanwhile, the woman of the house remains adamant that the Great War was caused by neither capitalism nor socialism – God, King nor Kaiser, but rather, she insists that the recent carnage in Europe during World War One was a direct result of, "the Italian Count that stole the heathen divinity out of a temple in Japan".

When I first read *Guests of the Nation*, I was too young and politically naive to grasp the full implications of the complexity and competing loyalties explored in O'Connor's story. But the sheer pain and heartbreak of a friendship tested by the demands of duty has resonated with me down through the years.

In 2003, as part of the national centenary celebrations of Frank O'Connor's birth, I was commissioned by RTÉ, the Irish National Broadcaster, to adapt *Guests of the Nation* for radio[19]. Thirty years had passed since I had first read the story, and I found myself revisiting and exploring O'Connor's work from the perspective of a writer rather than a reader – and there is a difference. Reading as a writer demands a more intense level of focus. It became a project of research as I found myself striving to get inside O'Connor's head in the hope that my adaptation would do justice not only to his storytelling and characterisations but also to his creative intent. And so, I set about deconstructing the story, every twist in the narrative was forensically examined, every character was held up to the light for scrutiny.

I was struck by the notion that this tale offered more than a nod of recognition to an earlier wave of guests to our nation – the Hiberno-Normans of the thirteenth century. Belcher and Hawkins, two English soldiers of fortune, find themselves in enemy hands as hostages. Their surnames are British and alien – Frank O'Connor makes a very conscious decision that these two soldiers would not have names that might identify them as sons or grandsons of Ireland, for to do so would set in place a very different dynamic and exploration. The realisation that Belcher and Hawkins were not of Irish immigrant stock was subtle but significant. Like their Hiberno-Norman [Anglo-Irish] counterparts of the thirteenth century, Belcher and Hawkins very quickly began to show signs of becoming 'more Irish than the Irish themselves' (ELLIS 1999). Unwittingly, they pay homage to pivotal moments in Irish history by learning the traditional dance steps such as *The Siege of Ennis* and *The Walls of Limerick*. This detail is

---

19 Guests of the Nation, this is the link to Cónal Creedon's radio play adaptation of O'Connor's short story https://www.youtube.com/watch?v=3EjX3Vu6dfY&t=930s

extremely noteworthy, as one of the early casualties of colonisation was the banning of Irish cultural practice including dance. The Statutes of Kilkenny (FOLEY 2017), passed into law in 1366, were specifically aimed at curtailing the behaviour of the Hiberno–Norman [Anglo–Irish] ruling class, rather than any intended suppression of the indigenous Irish. After two hundred years in situ in Ireland, the Hiberno–Normans [Anglo–Irish] were perceived by the London administration as being in danger of *going native*. Such an assimilation of culture was perceived as dangerous, seditious, interpreted as a potential divided loyalty or a conflict of interest, if not a direct threat to England from whence they came.

The friendship between sworn enemies is quickly established in the story, but commitment to duty brings the loyalty of friendship into sharp focus. When the order arrives from a higher authority that the British hostages are to be shot in reprisal for the execution of IRA volunteers in Dublin – the cold wind of reality sweeps across the bog, and the fragile utopian dream of peace among all men dissipates.

Selecting a name is a seminal moment in the life cycle of every fictional character. I found myself examining the names of the characters in this story in an attempt to uncover why O'Connor had opted to choose a particular name for a specific character. I will take this opportunity to present a brief analysis of the names attached to the various characters in *Guests of the Nation* with a view to understanding and unlocking their significance within O'Connor's story.

1. A Brief Analysis of Character Names

1.1 The Old Woman

The importance of the old woman in *Guests of the Nation* is often overlooked, maybe because O'Connor decided *not* to assign her character a name. Yet her presence looms large in the narrative. All the action unfolds in her cottage and on her land. The development of her very personal relationships with the IRA volunteers and the hostages, particularly Belcher and Jeremiah O'Donovan, acts as a barometer, tracking the changing mood within the story. So, I wondered why O'Connor had actively decided not to name a character of such significant presence.

There are a number of aspects regarding the old woman that are worthy of consideration. Historically, guerrilla and revolutionary armies don't have at their disposal the luxury of auxiliary resources such as barracks, canteens, hospitals, centres of recreation or prisons for incarceration of enemy prisoners. Guerrilla armies travel light, usually in small active service combat units, living off the land. Consequently, the support of a non-combatant public is essential. Active service units have the ability to appear as if out of nowhere from the general population and, having carried out a specific duty or action, they disappear back into the population. A network of discrete support systems is the lifeblood of survival and ultimate success for a guerrilla army.

That sense of a network of public support is referred to in *Guests of the Nation* when Hawkins reveals that, while they were prisoners of the 2nd Battalion, they had met a girl (Mary Brigid O'Connell) and her brother had a pair of Noble's socks. This creates a sense of captives being passed from one IRA unit to another. We are also given insight into an IRA active service unit travelling light through the countryside, stopping off at *safe houses* for rest and recreation – where they exchange news of the struggle and may even drop off prisoners and change into clean and dry clothes, eat a hot meal, sleep – before they move on.

A *safe house* is by definition a secret place of sanctuary. Anonymity, security, and isolation are the fundamental requirements of a safe house. In a hostage situation, as presented in *Guests of the Nation*, when enemy prisoners are incarcerated in a safe house, it demands more secrecy, more security, and a more long-term arrangement. In such a case, it is vital that the old woman is discreet, trustworthy and her loyalty to the cause must be unquestioning and unquestionable. Maybe it is precisely that sense of discretion and secrecy that O'Connor was implying when he decided not to reveal the name of the woman of the house — her name was on a need-to-know basis.

The old woman represents that section of society who supports the cause, but for many and various reasons decides not to participate in the military action. She represents the sympathiser, the enabler, the facilitator — that highly valued resource which is so essential to any guerrilla army in the field.

The old woman in this story is not politicised, she is not militarised. Her ill-informed analysis of World War One is revealing, particularly when she claims the war in Europe was caused by "the Italian Count that stole the heathen divinity out of a temple in Japan" (O'CONNOR 1931, 5). Despite her political naivety, she is wholeheartedly committed to the cause of Irish Independence and is without question willing to risk everything – her home, her land, her life by offering her cottage as a safe house for the IRA.

It is significant that O'Connor did not assign a name to the old woman. I believe she represents the faceless voice of Irish nationalism — that section of society who, for generations, has always had a deeply engrained loyalty to the cause of liberty, yet is not actively involved in the conflict. She represents that anonymous section of the population who offer crucial support to a guerrilla army in the field, yet whose names are seldom engraved on monuments or recorded in the history books[20].

---

20 In recent years, the research of historians is finding focus on many of these hitherto unknown, predominantly female activists – such as Sheila and Nora Wallace, Mary Bowels, Síobhan Creedon etc. who were active in the Cork area during the War of Independence.

1.2 JEREMIAH O'DONOVAN

Jeremiah O'Donovan is a gruff, uncompromising and seasoned IRA veteran. He is the officer in command of the younger IRA volunteers (Noble and Bonaparte). Clearly, Noble and Bonaparte are raw recruits. The task of guarding the hostages could very well be their first experience of active duty. Jeremiah O'Donovan spends most of his time barking out orders as he attempts to knock the young volunteers into shape.

Jeremiah O'Donovan is a dark character, with little time for small talk. He arrives without warning and leaves at short notice. His bitterness towards the British is extremely deep-rooted and unwavering. It is significant that the two young volunteers find it challenging to comprehend Jeremiah's coldness when it comes to the actual deed of executing the hostages.

O'Connor's choice of the name Jeremiah O'Donovan is a direct evocation of the Fenian leader, Jeremiah O'Donovan Rossa. The Fenians, also known as The Irish Republican Brotherhood (IRB), were hardcore militants who had survived the previous failed Irish Rebellion of the late 1800s. The Fenians (IRB) were the nucleus of militant nationalism during the early 1900s – a strictly secretive inner circle and driving force behind the 1916 Rising. They were the leaders, the planners and above all, they were responsible for *blooding* and bringing on the next generation of young militant nationalists (DORNEY 2017).

One Fenian in particular stands head and shoulders above all the rest, Jeremiah O'Donovan Rossa. His funeral was staged as a showcase of support – a call to arms for the many and various strands of Irish nationalism at home and abroad (MCGREEVY 2015). When Patrick Pearse gave his oration at Jeremiah O'Donovan Rossa's graveside (Hull) to a mass gathering of as many as 10,000 fully armed paramilitary Irish Volunteers (ROCHE 2015),

They Think they have foreseen everything,
But the fools, the fools, the fools!

They have left us our Fenian dead, and while Ireland holds these graves, Ireland unfree shall never be at peace.

the British authorities were left in no doubt that a rising was imminent.

There is no ambiguity in O'Connor's use of the name Jeremiah O'Donovan. The character in the story is an old Fenian (IRB). His role is to pass on the fire of nationalism to the next generation. He works at focusing the minds of the young recruits. His instruction to carry out the execution of the two British hostages is the defining test he will set the two young volunteers – Noble and Bonaparte.

Within the context of the story, Jeremiah O'Donovan could have quite simply executed the two British soldiers himself, but his insistence that the hostages should be executed by the two young IRA volunteers is clearly a test of their willingness to kill in cold blood, and an exercise in *blooding* the next generation. This is precisely the significance of Frank O'Connor's reference to Jeremiah O'Donovan Rossa – a figure who keeps the flame of insurrection burning long enough to influence the next generation of militant nationalists.

1.3 FEENEY

Feeney's presence in the narrative is intriguing. As a character, he seems totally insignificant and superfluous. One wonders why he is included in the text at all. He is often neglected, written off or ignored as a non-character in this story. Feeney's only appearance is on the fringes of the final scene. He doesn't speak. There is no sense of his physical appearance. He is always lurking in the shadows. He does not enter the light of the house. The reader is offered no glimpse of the physical features or the character of Feeney.

But if Jeremiah O'Donovan represents Jeremiah O'Donovan Rossa and the Fenian (IRB) influence on militant nationalism – then the case must be made that the elusive Feeney may be the most influential character of all. As his name suggests, Feeney could well be interpreted as the anglicisation of Na Fíníní, the Irish language word for The Fenians. The name Feeney also echoes the mythical Irish warrior class Na Fianna, and of course, Fianna Éireann, the Irish nationalist youth organisation established in 1909, most of whom went on to form the core of the Irish Volunteers during the 1916 Rising (HAY 2019).

We are told that Feeney is an "intelligence officer" which would place him as senior to Jeremiah O'Donovan in the chain of command. In the darkness of the bog, on the night of the execution – could it be the case that the silent Feeney, lurking in the shadows, is the judge and presiding senior officer in command. Is he present not only to ensure the executions are carried out in a correct and due military fashion, but also to appraise the actions and suitability of the young IRA volunteers (Noble and Bonaparte) for future duties.

Feeney's presence at the end of the story brings a great sense of menace and immediacy to the moment of execution. We can hear the urgency in Jeremiah O'Donovan's voice when he orders Noble to shoot Hawkins. We can feel his frustration when Noble refuses to carry out his duty. Could it be that Jeremiah's leadership is also the subject of appraisal by Feeney?

One might question the validity of including a character who does not speak, a character who remains concealed in the shadows. But it is a testament to O'Connor's literary brilliance that this unseen character, who lives in the shadows, offers such contextual depth and historical detail to the narrative, bringing a heightened reality to the core cast of characters who inhabit the spotlight.

1.4 BELCHER

Belcher is the older, mild-mannered and courteous British hostage. Curiously, his name seems at odds with his character. Belcher's personality is the very antithesis of the ill-mannered crudeness his name suggests. Described as a "gentleman" by the woman of the house, Belcher is presented as a philosophical man, a calming influence on the younger more impetuous IRA volunteers and Hawkins.

Belcher has lived a full life and seems comfortable with his own mortality – at ease with his impending fate. Belcher goes to his death with a certain resolve and detachment. It is significant that in his final words before execution he makes the point that he does not blame the volunteers who are about to carry out the deed, referring to them as "good lads", adding that he never quite understood the notion of duty.

1.5 Hawkins

Hawkins is the younger of the two British hostages. He is impetuous and argumentative and provides a perfect foil for Noble's character. Hawkins declares himself to be a communist and an atheist, and tends to be hawkish, combative and independent by nature. He represents the new generation who believe the next *war to end all wars* will not be nation versus nation, but rather it will be a clash of ideologies — the struggle between capitalism and socialism. Hawkins is not particularly committed to the British Army. He says that he would willingly desert (Ó RUAIRC 2011)[21] and join his newfound comrades (Noble and Bonaparte) in their fight for Irish independence. This is not necessarily just a ploy to save himself from execution, he genuinely considers the two young IRA volunteers as friends. It is apparent that he has found a kindred spirit in Noble, and there is a strong sense that he has misgivings about his role as a British soldier in Ireland.

1.6 Bonaparte

Bonaparte narrates *Guests of the Nation*. The story unfolds as a retro-spective personal retelling of Bonaparte's involvement in a traumatic

---

21 Commenting on British Soldiers deserting in Ireland, William McNamara 1st Batt. Mid Clare Brigade IRA said, "They were a decent body of men and the vast majority of them did not relish the particular class of soldering at which they were employed in Ireland. On pay nights, when a good number of them got a bit tipsy, they could be heard in the pubs in Ennis singing Irish rebel and Sinn Féin songs." Source: Bureau of Military History Witness Statement.

and tragic event during the Irish War of Independence. Bonaparte's character undergoes a dramatic shift, particularly in the context of his role in the execution of the two British soldiers, an event which ultimately had a profound effect on his life.

I believe his name, Bonaparte, was most likely a nickname given to him by his fellow IRA volunteer recruits – possibly a name he earned while participating in training camps. The implication being that he was viewed by his peers as a *little Napoleon* – gung-ho in training, a volunteer who had wholeheartedly embraced the demands, the trappings and challenges of guerrilla warfare, a young volunteer who craved action and the cut and thrust of battle, an enthusiastic volunteer who would carry out orders.

This is significant, because while the other young volunteer (Noble) is unable to shoot the hostages, Bonaparte steps up to the mark when duty calls. He has the steeliness that is required to pull the trigger and ultimately kill the hostage. Through this action, Bonaparte sets himself apart from Noble. Bonaparte has been *blooded*. The inferred narrative is that he will go on to become an active and full-blooded militant nationalist in the IRA.

Bonaparte's chilling statement at the end of the story, – "and anything that happened to me afterwards, I never felt the same about again" (MARTIN 1967 (2011), 86) – is often interpreted as an expression of his revulsion for the bloodletting of war. But alternatively, it seems to me, that having taken the step to pull the trigger and actually kill a British soldier in cold blood, there was no going back. His life and his commitment to the cause had risen to a higher level. Unlike Noble, who was unable to execute Hawkins, when Bonaparte pulled the trigger and killed the hostage, he learned something new about himself. Maybe that's why he "never felt the same about" anything that happened after that.

Guests of the Nation unfolds during the final months of the War of Independence, obviously the characters in the story do not have the gift of foresight and are not aware that, within a year, fuelled by the disputed terms of the treaty with the British, Ireland would erupt into full-blown civil war (KISSANE 2005).

The terms of the treaty between Ireland and England included partitioning the island of Ireland. Six counties of Ulster became known as Northern Ireland and remained within the jurisdiction of the United Kingdom. The treaty not only divided the island of Ireland, it also effectively split the IRA in two – Republicans and Free Staters. The Republican side vowing to continue the war against England to the bitter end, in an attempt to achieve an all-Ireland Republic. The Free State side opting to agree with the terms of the Treaty. This led to the inevitable clash between former comrades-in-arms, and so began the Irish Civil War (CLARKE, LITTON 2008).

Frank O'Connor identifies two individual and opposing personality traits in the young IRA volunteers, Noble and Bonaparte. When duty calls, Bonaparte is able to pull a trigger and kill. Noble on the other hand, is unable to kill. This subtle yet fundamental character difference could be a subliminal narrative signpost inserted into the narrative by O'Connor to suggest the potential loyalty choices of both volunteers in the impending Civil War. It is speculation on my part, but the character profile of Bonaparte, not least his ability to kill, leads me to believe that Bonaparte will align himself with the IRA hardliners and will continue the fight with the Republican side during the Civil War.

1.7 NOBLE

Noble is a young, hot-headed and argumentative IRA volunteer. Despite his characteristic bluff and bluster, it becomes apparent at the end of the story that the order to execute the two British soldiers was a test set by his commanding officer, Jeremiah O'Donovan, and Noble failed in his duty to carry out the order to kill. Noble would not have been aware that, within months of the Irish War of Independence, a civil war would sweep the land. It would be a brutal conflict of bloodletting between former comrades and once again Noble and Bonaparte's sense of loyalty and duty would be tested. Looking at Noble's character, it seems to me that he would support the peace terms of the treaty as negotiated by Michael Collins (HOPKINSON

2004), and most likely go on to become a supporter of the Free State rather than continue the struggle with the Republican side. Frank O'Connor deftly plants this subtle signpost to the future diverging lives of the two raw recruits. There is a sense that within a short time Noble might find himself fighting against his former comrade Bonaparte on the opposing side of the Irish Civil War. Could it be the case that Frank O'Connor is not only exploring the complication of a friendship between friend and foe, but also places a question over the friendship between friend and friend.

O'Connor's choice of the name Noble for this character is intriguing as the name seems at odds with the character presented in the story – although beneath his combative exterior we also see a mild, considered and emotional soul. Noble's quarrelsome exterior leads me to believe that his character is more brittle than hard.

When I first read this story over forty years ago, I was baffled by O'Connor's choice of such an obscure character name. It was a name that stood out. I had never come across the name Noble in Cork, or anywhere else for that matter – except in the pages of Frank O'Connor's story *Guests of The Nation*. I found it odd that such a quintessentially Cork writer would write a story so rooted in Cork, and yet select a name for a pivotal character with no context or reference to Cork.

In the course of my research, I found myself in the Cork City Archives thumbing through dusty old Irish Volunteer application forms from 1914. There, among that stack of maybe 2,000 documents, I was surprised to come across a young volunteer by the name of Noble – Noble Johnson. On closer inspection, I was amazed to find that this volunteer's address was – 11, Devonshire Street. Cork.

I live on Devonshire Street – 1, Devonshire Street to be precise. My family has traded on Devonshire Street for over a century. I knew instinctively that number eleven at the end of our street is now, was then and always has been Pa Johnson's Pub. Considering our two families have lived and traded on this street spanning a time frame that straddles two centuries and two millennia – it might be interesting to point out that generations of Creedons have stood at Johnson's

Irish Volunteer, Noble Johnson

bar counter, just as generations of Johnsons have stood at Creedon's shop counter.

So, purely in the interests of research, I visited Pa Johnson's pub, where my good friend and neighbour Barry Johnson is the current licensee. And having called a pint of Murphy's, I enquired as to how vigorously I'd have to shake his family tree for a Noble Johnson to fall out of its branches. Barry smiled, and he informed me that his grandfather, uncle and older brother were all named Noble. This kernel of information came as a great surprise to me. Noble was a name I had never known except as a character in *Guests of the Nation*, and there I was in my neighbour's pub, hearing for the first time about three individuals named Noble, all of whom had lived on my street.

I wondered whether it was possible that the character Noble in *Guests of the Nation* was inspired by Barry Johnson's grandfather. Frank O'Connor and Noble Johnson would have certainly known each other. Cork was a lot smaller back at the turn of the last century, the population and city boundary was only a fraction of what it is currently. Noble Johnson and Frank O'Connor were both members of the (Cork) Irish Volunteers. Both were from the Northside of the city. Johnson's pub was then and continues to be, a landmark hostelry in the city.

For me, the process of adapting Frank O'Connor's short story was never going to be just a matter of joining the narrative dots. Adaptation of another writer's work required that I find an emotional if not personal connection to the original. I like to think that there is a possibility of a connection between the character Noble the Republican in the story and Noble the publican on my street.

And so, before I put finger to keyboard, I broadened my research.

2. Art Imitates Life

In that twilight zone where art imitates life, there are many recorded incidents of hostage-taking by the IRA during the Irish War of Independence.

Frank O'Connor, a former member of the Irish Volunteers (IRA), would have been familiar with the numerous tales involving British hostages that were circulating at that time. Such incidents had become headline news, with daily updates reported in the press. Like present-day radio or television *soaps,* where the public is kept on tenterhooks as they await the latest developments – including the publication of photographs and extracts of highly personal, emotive and emotional love letters between hostages and their loved ones at home.[22]

Attempting to pinpoint the precise source of a writer's inspiration is near impossible, but tales of kidnapped British soldiers were very much part of the zeitgeist at that time. And of course, O'Connor's story would have brought its own influence and inspiration to bear on the work of future generations of writers – *The Hostage* and *An Giall* (1958) by Brendan Behan and Neil Jordan's film *The Crying Game* (1992) tackle similar themes and focus on the potential tragic outcome when friendships are formed between sworn enemies – specifically, in the context of British soldiers taken hostage by the IRA.

Certain aspects of these hostage-taking accounts displayed a great degree of similarity – captives being moved from safe house to safe house, and the responsibility for the custody of prisoners being handed from one IRA unit to another. Letter writing between captives and their loved ones became another common feature

---

22 An indication of the international media/press interest in the Major Compton-Smith story, full details of the kidnapping, incarceration, and execution of Major Compton-Smith, including transcripts of letters sent to his wife, his regiment, and the House of Commons debate feature in the Christchurch, New Zealand newspaper – The Star, Tuesday (18/05/26). https://paperspast.natlib.govt.nz/imageserver/newspapers/ P29pZD1UUzE5MjYwNTE4LjEuNiZnZnXRwZGY9dHJ1ZQ== (03/2021).

as well as socialising between captives and captors, including card playing, singsongs and dancing – which inevitably brought about the complicating dilemma of friendships formed between enemies during wartime.

The kidnapping of Brigadier-General Cuthbert Lucas stands out as one of the more bizarre accounts. Brigadier-General Lucas was Officer in Command of the 16th Infantry Brigade, stationed at Fermoy Barracks in East Cork. He holds the dubious honour of being the most senior-ranking British army officer taken captive by the IRA (MCGREEVY 2020B).

Liam Lynch of the East Cork 2nd Battalion IRA devised a plan to capture a high-ranking British officer with a view to holding him hostage in exchange for IRA prisoners who were facing execution at Victoria Barracks in Cork City (RYAN 2012). The opportunity to put the plan into action arose on 26th June 1920, when Brigadier-General Lucas, Colonel Danford of the Royal Artillery and Colonel Tyrrell of the Royal Engineers were spotted fly fishing on the River Bride near the town of Fermoy in East Cork. Word was relayed back to Liam Lynch, who made his move, and a plan was hastily put into action.

A unit of East Cork 2nd Battalion IRA made their way to the riverbank and took the three British officers captive at gunpoint. The hostages were transported from the scene in two waiting cars (API PARLIAMENT, UK – HANSARD 1803–2005, 28 JUNE 1920). But the abduction was not without incident. Colonel Danford and Brigadier-General Lucas, who were travelling in the second getaway car, made an attempt to escape. In a botched effort at overpowering the driver, a fight broke out causing the car to career off the road and crash. The fist fight which began inside the moving vehicle spilled out onto the road and erupted in a full-scale brawl between the IRA volunteers and the British army officers. The lead car carrying Colonel Tyrrell returned to the scene of the skirmish to find Colonel Danford had broken free and had made a run for freedom. Order was only restored when two gunshots rang out and Colonel Danford fell to the road wounded. Liam Lynch decided that Colonel Tyrrell would be left behind to care for Colonel Danford, and the IRA hightailed it with their prized possession, Brigadier-General Lucas (MURPHY 2020A).

When news of the kidnapping reached Fermoy Barracks, a massive manhunt was mounted right across the Province of Munster. Two nights later the East Kent Regiment ransacked and looted the nearby town of Fermoy in reprisal for the kidnapping of the Brigadier-General. The New York Times reported on 28th June 1920,

> Barracks and camp were immediately alarmed, and all soldiers turned out of bed. Soldiers of an artillery battery mounted their horses and numerous parties of fully equipped troops in motor cars, scoured the country for miles around all day and all night. But the general had vanished completely. (CARROLL 2010, 50)

A fascinating photograph of Brigadier-General Lucas (seated centre) during his captivity. Seen here in the company of his captors: Paddy Brennan, Michael Brennan, James Brennan and Joe Keane of the East Clare Brigade IRA. Brigadier-General Lucas wearing the suit bought for him by his captors in Limerick. The photograph beautifully captures the recreational and comfortable atmosphere that existed between friend and foe. Note: Commandant Michael Brennan of the East Clare Brigade IRA (2nd from left) with revolver in trousers belt. Courtesy of Cork Public Museum.

And so began an intriguing and highly dangerous game of cat and mouse as Brigadier-General Lucas was moved from safe house to safe house through North Cork, Limerick, Tipperary and Clare – always one step ahead of the British authorities.

A peculiar aspect of Lucas' time in captivity was his insistence that he should receive a bottle of whiskey every day. As an officer this was his statutory prisoner-of-war allowance. His request was duly honoured. The whiskey intensified a social aspect to his incarceration. As one would expect, friendships developed — as related by Jack Horgan of the Shannon Social History Project.

> He (Brigadier-General Lucas) was a very affable sort of man who was easy to get on with. They played cards with him. He was particularly good at poker. He also played bridge and they taught him to play Forty-fives. He also liked his whiskey and had plenty of help drinking it. The trouble was that they couldn't keep him. He used to drink a bottle of whiskey every day and he cleaned them out at poker. (HORGAN 2011)

Shortly after Lucas was taken hostage, his wife, Poppy Lucas, gave birth to their first child. He was granted permission by the IRA, on compassionate grounds, to write home to his wife. In due course, Poppy replied to her husband, she simply addressed her letters to: General Lucas, c/o THE IRA. Ireland (MCGREEVY 2020B). There followed a relay of letters between Lucas and his wife which are currently held in the Lucas family archive. Their correspondence makes for fascinating reading. They contain many references to how well he was treated by the IRA, including accounts of playing croquet and tennis, games of cards that stretched late into the night, fishing expeditions on the River Shannon and days spent helping farmers in the fields "to save the hay" (MURPHY 2020B).

There were a number of farcical escapades during his incarceration, including a shopping trip into Limerick city to buy clothes for the Brigadier-General who was still in his fishing attire since his abduction.[23] There's also the amusing anecdotal tale of Brigadier-General Lucas and his IRA captors salmon poaching on the River Shannon in Co. Limerick. Seemingly, Lucas expressed concern that they might be caught fishing illegally by the river bailiffs. His concerns were laid to rest when he was reassured that the IRA volunteer rowing the boat was in fact the local river bailiff (BRENNAN 2012).

Lucas was held hostage for over a month, but the IRA became frustrated due to the British lack of interest in facilitating a prisoner exchange. The incarceration of Lucas was costing the IRA heavily in manpower and resources. It has been suggested that Lucas' skilful card playing and his capacity for the consumption of alcohol may have played a part in the IRA's decision to release him unharmed. Eventually, on 30th July, Commandant Michael Brennan of the East Clare Brigade IRA decided that Lucas would be allowed to escape (BRENNAN 1980).

Brigadier-General Lucas' release by the IRA was not the end of the story. It is on record that he made his way on foot to the RIC barracks in the nearby village of Pallas Green, Co. Limerick. There he had a bath and a change of clothes. He then wrapped the clothes he had been wearing and instructed that they be posted simply to the address: c/o The IRA. The parcel eventually reached the IRA in East Cork with a note attached that simply reads:

> To the Sinn Féiners, or to the IRA, with compliments of General Lucas.
> (MURPHY 2020B)

This anecdote of purchasing clothes for General Lucas and his decision to return the clothes to the IRA on his release has special resonance with the Frank O'Connor's story *Guests of the Nation*. For me, it highlights the significance of Hawkins relating to Bonaparte that he had met Mary Brigid O'Connell while held captive by the 2nd Battalion IRA, a girl whose brother had a pair of Bonaparte's socks.

---

23 https://roundaboutshannon.clareheritage.org/new-contributions/the-capture-of-brigadier-general-lucas

It identifies that very basic requirement of a supply of fresh, clean and dry clothes, for an IRA active service unit on the move. Clearly, Brigadier-General Lucas was aware of the importance that a supply of clothes might be to his former captives and so he duly returned the suit they had bought for him.

Another extraordinary episode unfolded as General Lucas was on his journey home to Fermoy Barracks in Co. Cork from Pallas Green, Co. Limerick. By pure chance, that very same day, the 3rd Tipperary Brigade IRA under Sean Tracy had planned to ambush the mail convoy, unaware that Lucas, released a day earlier by the East Clare Brigade IRA, was on board.

The convoy rolled into the IRA ambush near Oola in Co. Tipperary. An intense firefight ensued and within a short time, two British soldiers lay dead on the road and three others were wounded. When the gunfire ceased and the smoke cleared, it was found that General Lucas had survived the attack — once again, the fickle finger of fate intervened and deemed that Lucky Lucas would live to tell the tale.

The IRA failed to secure a prisoner exchange with the British authorities, but the kidnapping of such a high-ranking officer and their efficiency in concealing his whereabouts across a number of counties was a great morale boost for the Irish Volunteers. The kidnapping made international news headlines – it was reported that the then Secretary of State for War, Winston Churchill was "purple with rage" (MCGREEVY 2020). Meanwhile, a satirical street ballad, *Where Did General Lucas Go?*, aimed at taunting British soldiers, became popular around the towns and villages of North Cork. But most significantly, at a time when the British authorities were actively portraying the Irish Volunteers as murder gangs and indiscriminate killers, General Lucas' accounts of the friendships he had formed during his captivity became a source of embarrassment. In particular, on Tuesday 29th June 1920, *The Irish Bulletin* published an extract from a letter to his wife, in which Lucas stated that his captors were "delightful people", and he went on to say, "I was treated as a gentleman by gentlemen". Lucas reaffirmed these sentiments when he got back to Fermoy Barracks. He addressed his troops and admonished those who had committed outrages and atrocities in retaliation for his abduction — insisting that the troops under his command had shown "an overzealous display".

Where did General Lucas Go?

Can anybody tell me where did General Lucas go?
He may be down in Mitchelstown or over in Mallow?
He's somewhere in the county Cork but this I want to know.
Can anybody tell me where did General Lucas go?

'Twas on a Sunday morning out a fishing he did go.
And when he had his fishing done he was caught by you know who
They said you'll have to come with us or down you will go.
For that's the way we'll treat you where the blarney roses grow.

There's good men down in Galway and the same in county Clare.
But the likes of these young Cork men you won't find anywhere.
They treated me so kindly if they only let me go.
I'd promise to stop reprisals where the blarney roses grow.[24]

The kidnapping of Brigadier-General Lucas had an air of an Ealing Comedy slapstick adventure, but the same cannot be said for all such incidents. There are several recorded examples of strong bonds of friendship formed between friend and foe that came to a profoundly tragic end when duty called, and the inevitability of execution had to be carried out.

During my research, the kidnapping of another senior British officer, Major Geoffrey Lee Compton-Smith, attracted my attention. Not only because of the striking similarities to the narrative of *Guests of the Nation*, but Major Compton-Smith had been held captive in Donoughmore, Co. Cork – the birthplace of Frank O'Connor's mother. O'Connor had many happy childhood memories of visits to his extended maternal family in Donoughmore – it is noteworthy

---

24 I wish to direct the reader to, Kidnapping of General Lucas by Pauline Murphy – online article in Headstuff (June 2020) https://headstuff.org/culture/history/irish-history-history/where-did-general-lucas-go-the-kidnapping-of-general-cuthbert-lucas/

that he adopted his mother's family name (O'Connor) as his pen name in favour of his paternal surname, O'Donovan.

The fictional tale explored in *Guests of the Nation* presents many close similarities to the true story of Major Compton-Smith, who was taken hostage by the IRA and held in exchange for the release of four IRA volunteers facing execution in Victoria Barracks, Cork. Considering Frank O'Connor's family connections to the locality of Donoughmore and his membership of the Irish Volunteers, it is highly probable that O'Connor would have been very familiar with the key individuals and locations associated with the tragic events surrounding this particular kidnapping.

It was reported at the time that Major Compton-Smith had been on a landscape painting excursion to Blarney on the outskirts of Cork City when an IRA unit chanced upon him. In an interview published by *The Cork Examiner* on 4th June 1921, Compton-Smith's wife, Gladys, picks up the story:

> Sketching was a favourite amusement of my husband, and he had gone to Blarney, presumably to sketch the castle, when he fell into the hands of the Sinn Féiners. I received a letter from him written the next day, in which he said, – while away sketching yesterday I had the misfortune to get held up by the IRA. I am now a prisoner but being very well treated. I have no doubt I shall get out of this scrape as I have got out of others. There is nothing to worry about.

But the painting excursion theory is unconvincing. It seems highly unlikely that a senior British Army Intelligence Officer would be ambling around the countryside painting landscapes in a known IRA stronghold at a time when the War of Independence was at its height and raging out of control. The previous six months had seen a sharp escalation in IRA unilateral attacks on British army personnel. General Strickland, Officer in Command of the Southern Division at Victoria Barracks in Cork, had issued strict guidelines regarding the security of senior staff and officers.

Local lore in Donoughmore has it that Major Compton-Smith had been lured to Blarney Station in a honey-trap to meet a nurse.

This assertion was given some credence when Sir Harmood-Banner stated in The British House of Commons,

Major Compton-Smith left his home in mufti [civilian clothing] to meet the monthly nurse.

(API PARLIAMENT UK – HANSARD 1803-2005, 23 JUNE 1921)

But Compton-Smith's reason for being in Blarney that day was irrelevant, be it his love of art or an affair of the heart. We now know that no nurse was waiting on the platform when the Major stepped from the train. Instead, he was greeted by an active service unit of the local IRA under Frank Busteed and was taken prisoner. Major General Strickland, Officer in Command of Victoria Barracks, Cork, was subsequently contacted and informed that Compton-Smith would be released unharmed in exchange for four IRA prisoners who were due to be executed on 28th April 1921. And so began the deeply moving story of Major Compton-Smith's captivity.

Some years ago, I and two friends of mine, John Borgonovo and Dan Breen, were invited by the descendants of the IRA volunteers involved in the kidnapping of Major Compton-Smith to visit the key locations where he had been held hostage.

It was one of those magical days that found its own momentum, and as we travelled through the countryside, each turn of the road opened up a vista into the past. It was a day of song and story, a day where new friendships were made, and old friendships were copper-fastened. It was a day of lore, a day of – *what if?* It was an emotional and visceral day where painful memories of generations past were laid bare and in some cases laid to rest. I will attempt to recount my thoughts and memories of that day to the best of my recollection.[25]

25 I wish to direct the reader to (Documentary On One: I Am To Be Shot) a podcast documentary, which was made by UCC student, Saoirse Sheehan, from Donoughmore in 2021. (https://www.rte.ie/radio/radio1/highlights/1243763-documentary-on-one-i-am-to-be-shot/)

We were met at the railway station in the village of Blarney, just as Compton-Smith had been met by Frank Busteed and his IRA unit that fateful day back on 16th April 1921. We travelled in convoy along a maze of disorientating back roads and boreens, our driver pointing out significant locations along the way. We stopped off at various ambush sites and a string of safe houses that had held Compton-Smith. He shared details of another more controversial event: the kidnapping and execution of Mrs. Lindsay and her chauffeur, Mr. James Clarke (GORDON 2015) – which, incidentally, had also been carried out by the local IRA under the command of Frank Busteed just a few short weeks prior to the taking of Major Compton-Smith. We were also told the fascinating story of a Rolls Royce Silver Ghost armoured car, known locally as the Moon Car, an IRA war machine of mythical status. We were brought to the farmyard where the Moon Car had been buried after the Free State Government put up a bounty of £10,000 for information leading to its whereabouts (National Museum of Ireland). It struck me that every twist and turn of the road through this beautiful tranquil, green and leafy countryside had a story to tell of a violent and bloody past.

Eventually we reached our destination – a side-track at a bend on the road. There we parked the cars. The remainder of the journey was made on foot, along a hillside track to the isolated cottage where Major Compton-Smith spent his final days.

The rain was driving hard, so we took shelter in the derelict cottage. Lightning flashed and thunder crashed, as if nature had presented us with a magnificent theatrical backdrop for that most evocative of days. Standing there, looking out across the valley, there was talk of the people of Donoughmore and Major Compton-Smith. The conversation was peppered with memories that had been handed down through the various families from generation to generation. Gradually, the story emerged of how a series of catastrophic events in another part of the county had led to the kidnapping of Major Compton-Smith.

In February 1921 an IRA ambush in Mourneabbey near Mallow, Co. Cork went badly wrong. Four volunteers died as a result of

The Cottage in Donoughmore where Major Compton-Smith was held hostage before his execution by the IRA. Courtesy of Denise Sheehan.

the incident, and several were taken prisoner. Two of the prisoners, Patrick Ronayne and Thomas Mulcahy, were court-martialled and sentenced to death. The executions were to take place on 28th April 1921. Then a few days later another IRA flying column found themselves surrounded in a farmhouse near Clonmult in East Cork. There are several accounts of what happened at Clonmult – but the only certainty is that 12 volunteers were shot dead, and a number were taken prisoner – Maurice Moore and Patrick O'Sullivan were court-martialled and also scheduled to be executed on 28th April 1921. With four young volunteers facing execution, the IRA decided they would take a senior British Officer hostage to be held in exchange for the release of the four volunteers. Major Compton-Smith was that hostage, and so the waiting game began.

In an interview with *The Cork Examiner* on 4th June 1921, Gladys Compton-Smith quoted from another letter she had received from her husband which highlights the social and informal nature of his incarceration.

I am still going strong and write this lying on a heap of hay in a barn. It has been most interesting to compare notes with the Sinn Féiners. Last night I had a discussion with a lot of them representing different ranks, and rebels with various grades of education were sitting round the cottage fire. I was single-handed among many. Some of them were very bitter against us, but they treated me most fairly. The night ended up with a song in which I joined in most heartily. (THE STAR 1926)[26]

It becomes apparent that, like Frank O'Connor's short story, a deep friendship and mutual respect developed between Major Compton-Smith and his captors. The deepening relationship is highlighted in a letter to his regiment written shortly before he was executed.

I intend to die with forgiveness for those who are carrying out this deed. I should like my death to lessen rather than increase the bitterness which exists between England and Ireland. I have been treated with great kindness, and during my captivity have learned to regard the Sinn Féiners rather as mistaken idealists than as a murder gang. (O'HALPIN, Ó CORRÁIN 2020, 398–399)

Once again, the heightened emotion of the time becomes evident in what has become known as the 'Shot In An Hour's Time' letter, which Major Compton-Smith wrote to his wife, Gladys. In it, as a dying wish, he asks that his watch be given to the IRA volunteer charged with the duty of carrying out his execution – and describes his executioner as a gentleman.

26 As a measure of the international interest in Major Compton-Smith story, full details of the kidnapping, incarceration and execution of Major Compton-Smith, including letters sent to his wife, his regiment, and the House of Commons debate feature in the Christchurch, New Zealand newspaper – The Star, Tuesday (18th May 26). This is an extract of a letter sent by Major Compton-Smith to his wife Gladys as reported in this article. https://paperspast.natlib. govt.nz/imageserver/newspapers/ P29pZD1UUzE5MjYwNTE4LjEuNiZnZXRwZGY9dHJ1ZQ== (03/2021).

ART IMITATING LIFE IMITATING DEATH

Major Geoffrey Compton-Smith with his wife Gladys on their wedding day.
(Courtesy of Rupert Peploe of The Compton-Smith Family Archive)

Dearest, Gladys,

your hubby will die with your name on his lips, your face before his eyes, and he will die like an Englishman and a soldier. I cannot tell you sweetheart how much it is to me to leave you alone – nor how little to me personally to die – I have no fear, only the utmost, greatest and tenderest love to you, and my sweet little Anne. I leave my cigarette case to the Regiment, my miniature medals to my father – whom I have implored to befriend you in everything – and my watch to the officer who is executing me because I believe him to be a gentleman and to mark the fact that I bear him no malice for carrying out what he sincerely believes to be his duty. Goodbye, my darling, my own. Tender, tender farewells and kisses. Your own, Geoff (KENEFICK 2011)[27]

Of course, Compton-Smith would not have been aware that his alleged meeting with the monthly nurse at Blarney Station had been discussed in the British Parliament and the details were reported in the British Press – his alleged intended liaison with the nurse would have been a source of great public humiliation for his wife and family.

And so, I found myself with the descendants of those who had held Major Compton-Smith hostage – sheltering from the elements in this derelict hillside cottage. Almost a hundred years had passed, yet the memory was visceral and the mood sombre. The rain stopped, the wind eased, and, with the lull in the weather, our guides decided to take the opportunity to lead us up the winding track to the place of Major Compton-Smith's execution. As we made our way along there was talk of mundane but no less important matters: the land, the weather, sheep and cattle. It occurred to me that not a lot had changed around Donoughmore since the time Compton-Smith came and lived among these people. The land continued to be farmed

27 This final letter between Major Compton-Smith and his wife Gladys, was given the name "Shot In An Hour's Time" by Sir Harmood-Banner, when he read the full transcript of the letter to the House of Commons (01/06/1921). The emotional content of the letter was immediately seized upon by the international media, propelling the story of Major Compton-Smith's kidnapping and execution onto the world stage. See https://historic-graves.com/story/major-geoffrey-lee-compton-smith.

by generations of the same families – back as far as anyone could remember. This landscape had been shaped by the people, just as much as the people had been shaped by the landscape. These people were not a professionally trained military machine, they had little by way of weaponry or resources. For generations, they had eked out a living on small holdings. Their ancestors had survived the Great Irish Famine, but many of their neighbours would have perished in a national disaster, not a natural disaster – and the accusatory finger of guilt was pointed at their overlords, the British administration. Little had changed over the generations, these people continued to plough, sow and harvest – for not to do so would have meant that they and their families would go hungry. First and foremost, the people of Donoughmore were farmers. Clearly, they had been willing to fight and die for the cause of Irish Independence. And just like so many other villages, parishes and townlands across the land, the people of Donoughmore had stood up to one of the most powerful colonising and warlike nations on the planet – and surprisingly, they were victorious.

I wondered if Major Compton-Smith had made similar observations during his time among the people of Donoughmore. He had recently returned from the mindless human carnage and destruction of World War One, it must have been a surreal experience to find himself held captive, with his life in the balance, in a rural townland such as Donoughmore. Ironically, from Compton-Smith's point of view, Donoughmore was as much part of the British countryside as Kent or Dorset. Here the main activity of any particular day would be centred around domestic rural pursuits: milking cows, feeding chickens, baking bread. It is difficult to comprehend the confused emotions he must have experienced, to find himself sitting at a farmhouse kitchen table sharing meals with a family, playing cards, singing songs – living as a guest of the enemy. This country cottage was a busy hub in a rebel stronghold. And yet all around the sound of domesticity; the sound of children playing, cattle lowing, cats and their kittens lapping up saucers of milk, the sheep dog barking and putting the run on the phantoms of the night, and the beady-eyed

Public Protest execution of Irish prisoners. Courtesy Cork City Museum.

chickens pecking at the window. In his letters to his wife, Major Compton-Smith refers to the social aspect of the revolutionary gatherings at the fireside, the comings and goings of gunmen to the house:

> a lot of them representing different ranks, and rebels with various grades of education were sitting round the cottage fire.

The Major must have re-evaluated his indoctrination about the Sinn Féiners and questioned their portrayal as bloodthirsty murder gangs. Did he conclude that his hosts, these hillside farmers were just ordinary people caught up in the events of extraordinary times?

Such were the thoughts that filled my head as we wound our way along the hillside track. When we finally reached the place where Major Compton-Smith met his doom, the conversation turned to the events that led to his execution. Among those present, there was a general sense of seething anger at the "800 years of oppression" that had been inflicted on the people of Ireland by the English. A particular and palpable fury was reserved for the British authorities whose inaction during the Spring of 1921 had placed the local people in an impossible moral dilemma – faced with no alternative but to execute this enemy who had become a friend. It was suggested by one of our party that – if the British had only met them halfway and commuted the death sentence of the four Irish Volunteers to life imprisonment, Compton-Smith would have been released unharmed.

In the context of that time, appeasement was not on the British agenda. If anything, hostility was escalating. Shootings, ambushes became the order of the day in an ever-increasing cycle of violence fuelled by reprisal and counter-reprisal. Only a few weeks previously, on the morning of 23rd March, 1921, a safe house at Ballycannon on the northside of Cork City was surrounded by a large force of Black and Tans. Volunteers: Thomas Dennehy, Jeremiah Mullane, Michael Sullivan, Daniel Crowley, William Deasy and Daniel Murphy, members of the Blarney Street Company of the IRA were found sleeping in a shed – all were shot dead.

Major Compton-Smith's fate was sealed on 28th April 1921, when Patrick Ronayne, Thomas Mulcahy, Maurice Moore and Patrick O'Sullivan were executed at Victoria Barracks in Cork City. Two days later, on 30th April 1921, Compton-Smith was taken to the very spot where we were standing in that lonely bog on a hillside near Donoughmore – he died by a single bullet to the head.

The details of his execution are recorded in the Bureau of Military History Witness Statement by Maurice Brew.

When removed to the place of execution, he placed his cigarette case in his breast pocket of his tunic and asked that after his death it should be sent to his regiment. He then lighted a cigarette and said that when he dropped the cigarette, it could be taken as a signal by the execution squad to open fire. (BHM 1951)

Before we departed, one of our hosts stepped forward and spoke of the respect and friendship that had been forged between Compton-Smith and the local people of Donoughmore. Like an echo from the past, the emotions and feelings had survived through the generations right to the present day. We were reminded that 1920 was a time of war. A list of atrocities that occurred throughout the centuries of abuse, poverty, starvation and death during the eight hundred years of English occupation were recalled like stepping-stones through time. Then, just as in the closing moments of Frank O'Connor's story, following a moment of reflection, he proceeded to recite a decade of the Rosary – *as gaeilge*[28] – for the repose of the souls of Major Compton-Smith and the executed IRA volunteers: Patrick Ronayne, Thomas Mulcahy, Maurice Moore and Patrick O'Sullivan. Instinctively, we all joined in.

There is a postscript to the tragic tale. In 1922 Ireland had become the battleground of a bloody civil war. Michael Collins, the chief negotiator of the Anglo-Irish Treaty, and now the leader of the Irish Free State who were locked in a spiralling cycle of violence with Irish Republican forces (COOGAN 2015)[29], made several attempts on behalf of Compton-Smith's family to find, exhume and repatriate his remains to England. But the horrors of the Irish War of Independence had been overtaken by the more poignant and personalised bloodletting of the Irish Civil War. With former comrades taking up arms against each other, the country was once again plunged into turmoil. Major Compton-Smith's body lay buried in an IRA stronghold, making it next to impossible for the Irish Free State authorities to retrieve his remains.

---

28 Translation: 'as gaeilge': 'In the Irish Language'
29 Michael Collins was an Irish revolutionary leader during the War of Independence, a leading figure in the early 20th century Irish struggle for independence. He was Chairman of the Provisional Government of the Irish Free State during the Irish Civil War. Because of disputes arising from the agreed peace treaty with Britain, the Civil War unfolded as a particularly personalised bloodletting between the Irish Free State and their former comrades in the IRA.

In his correspondence with Gladys, the wife of Major Compton-Smith, Michael Collins outlined the difficulties he faced in locating her husband's remains:

Dear Madam,
I beg to acknowledge receipt of your letter of 21st April. You will understand that in the present circumstances here in Ireland, it is extremely difficult to attend to matters of this kind. Even though it is not possible to secure all the information I should like to secure for you, you may rely on me to keep the matter in my mind with a view to giving all remaining details, and securing, if necessary, the transfer of the remains as soon as conditions become restored here.
(KENEFICK 2011)

And such is the tragedy of Civil War, within a few months, Michael Collins was dead — killed in an ambush set by his former IRA comrades at Béal na Bláth, just 15 miles west of Donoughmore.

When peace was eventually restored to the land, Compton-Smith's body was recovered. On Friday, 15th March 1926 *The Cork Examiner* reported:

The remains were located in Barracharing wood and brought in a lead covered coffin to Collins Barracks[30] – they will remain there pending the receipt of instructions as to their removal to England.

In the intervening six years, Major Compton-Smith's widow had remarried and was living in Italy as Gladys Mary Peterson – the wife of Major Guy Lansberry Peterson. Protracted negotiations took place between the Irish Free State and the Compton-Smith family but, for some unspecified reason, the family declined the opportunity to bring his remains home to England. In April 1926, Major Compton-Smith

30 In the intervening four years since the Civil War had ended [1922 – 1926], Victoria Barracks in Cork City, which had been the centre of British Military administration, was re-named Collins Barracks by the Irish Free State Government – in memory of Michael Collins.

was finally laid to rest in Fort Carlisle Military Cemetery, Whitegate, Co. Cork, where he is interred to the present day. At the base of his headstone is a bronze wreath with a short inscription from his daughter Anne:

Major G L Compton-Smith D.S.O.
With Love from Anne. (KENEFICK 2011)

3. In Conclusion

That day I spent as a guest of the people of Donoughmore is indelibly imprinted on my memory. The mood was solemn and dignified in accordance with honouring the memory of past generations. Having paid our respects, we made our way back down that lonely hillside track and regrouped at a local farmhouse. There, a fine spread and a blazing turf fire awaited us. The talk was of tales of the townland, times past and hopes for the future, and as afternoon drifted towards evening we sang songs – I believe I may have given a verse or two of the *Lonely Woods at Upton*.[31]

Our reason for gathering that day was never too far from our minds. Someone mentioned Major Compton-Smith's watch. *The Cork Examiner* of 15th March 1926 published a letter sent by Major Compton-Smith to his wife Gladys which had been written just moments prior to his execution. In it the Major expressed as a dying wish that his watch would be given to the IRA volunteer charged with the duty of carrying out the execution.

> and my watch to the officer who is executing me because I believe him to be a gentleman and to mark the fact that I bear him no malice for carrying out what he sincerely believes to be his duty. (BENNETT 2010 [1959], 191)

There was general agreement that the gifting of such a personal possession to his executioner was a clear indication of the genuine affection and meeting of minds that had occurred between two sworn enemies. When asked about the current whereabouts of the watch the reply was vague, but I understood it was still in the possession of a family in Donoughmore, not too far from the kitchen table where we were sitting. And there was something very reassuring in the realisation that Major Compton-Smith's watch was not displayed

---

31 Lonely Woods Of Upton, commemorates an IRA ambush on a train at Upton Station in North Cork. This is the link to Sean Dunphy singing the song. https://www.youtube.com/watch?v=5WpOoil9eB8

as a trophy of war but rather held as a treasured personal gift from a friend.

There was talk of the very public humiliation endured by Gladys Compton-Smith when it was announced from the floor of the British Parliament that her husband had not been on a landscape painting expedition, but rather, had gone to Blarney to meet a nurse. We wondered whether the decision by the Compton-Smith family not to repatriate his body to England, and the omission of his wife's name on the bronze wreath at the Major's headstone, was in response to his alleged indiscretion with the nurse at Blarney Station? Could it be the case that sometimes all is not fair in love and war? Such are the fascinating speculations of love and lore.

The many and varied tales of British soldiers taken hostage by the IRA are invaluable to historians and academics. They offer a precise and factually detailed account of Ireland and the inner-workings of IRA active service units at the height of the War of Independence – on the cusp of the Civil War. But the genius of Frank O'Connor's fiction is found in the depth and complexity of the characters he creates – the story as it unfolds is but a backdrop from which a fascinating cast of full-bodied characters come alive. *Guests of the Nation* brings us on an emotional rollercoaster journey that leads directly to the beating heart and very soul of rural Ireland. O'Connor invites the reader into a magical world where history and story go hand in hand and fact and fiction dovetail together seamlessly without contradiction or contrivance.

Works Cited

BENNETT Richard (2010 [1959]), *The Black and Tans*, Barnsley, Pen & Sword Books Limited.

BRENNAN John (2014), "Interview", in *Shannon 'Between Old World and New World'. A Social History Project"*, Analysis and Development by Olive Carey On behalf of Dúchas na Sionna (Clare County Library Dúchas na Sionna), https://www.clarelibrary.ie/eolas/coclare/history/Shannon%20Social%20History%20Project.pdf (03/2021).

BRENNAN Michael (1980), *The War in Clare, 1911–1921: Personal Memoirs of the Irish War of Independence*, Dublin-Newbridge, Four Courts Press-Irish Academic Press.

CARROLL Aideen (2010), *Sean Moylan: Rebel Leader*, Cork, Mercier Press Ltd.

CLARKE Kathleen, Litton Helen, eds (2008), *Kathleen Clarke: Revolutionary Woman*, Dublin, O'Brien Press.

COLLINS Stephen (2014), "One Hundred Years since John Redmond Committed Ireland to the First World War", *The Irish Times*, 2 August, https://www.irishtimes.com/news/politics/one-hundred-yearssince-john-redmond-committed-ireland-to-the-first-world-war-1.1885199 (03/2021).

COOGAN T.P. (2015), *Michael Collins: A Biography*, London, Arrow Books.

COSTELLO Peter (2014), "Revisionism in Ireland. A Wrong-Headed View of Revisionism", *The Irish Catholic*, 2 January, https://www.irishcatholic.com/a-wrong-headed-view-of-revisionism (03/2021).

DANA (1970), "All Kinds of Everything", *Eurovision Song Contest*, Amsterdam, https://www.youtube.com/watch?v=8xmnd3uiK_Y (03/2021).

DORNEY John (2017), "The Fenians: An Overview", *The Irish Story*, 7 March, https://www.theirishstory.com/2017/03/07/the-fenians-an-overview/#.X6VGTi-l3_8 (03/2021).

DUNPHY Sean. "Woods of Upton", https://www.youtube.com/watch?v=5WpOoi-l9eB8 (03/2021).

ELLIS S.G. (1999), "More Irish Than the Irish Themselves?", *History Ireland 1, 7*, https://www.historyireland. com/20th-century-contemporary-history/more-irish-than-the-irish-themselves (03/2021).

FERGUSON Amanda (2015), "Council votes to rename Londonderry as Derry", *The Irish Times*, 24 July, https://www.irishtimes.com/news/politics/council-votes-to-rename-londonderry-as-derry-1.2296065 (03/2021).

FOLEY Áine (2017), "Statutes of Kilkenny", *The Encyclopaedia of Medieval Literature in Britain*, 3 August, https://onlinelibrary.wiley.com/doi/abs/10.1002/9781118396957.wbemlb525 (03/2021).

FOY Michael, BARTON Brian (2011), *The Easter Rising*, Stroud, The History Press.

GORDON Cécile (2015), "The Case of Mrs. Lindsay", *History Ireland 23, 5*, https://www.historyireland.com/volume-23/the-case-of-mrs-lindsay (03/2021).

HAY Marnie (2019), Na Fianna Éireann and the Irish Revolution, 1909-23: Scouting for Rebels, Manchester, Manchester UP.

HENEY Michael (2020), *The Arms Crisis Of 1970: the Plot that Never Was*, London, Apollo.

HOPKINSON Michael (2004), *Green Against Green – The Irish Civil War: a History of the Irish Civil War, 1922-1923*.

HOGAN Jack, Hogan Nuala (2014), "Interview", in *Shannon 'Between Old World and New World'. A Social History Project", Analysis and Development by Olive Carey On behalf of Dúchas na Sionna* (Clare County Library Dúchas na Sionna), https://www.clarelibrary.ie/eolas/coclare/history/Shannon%20Social%20History%20Project.pdf (03/2021).

HULL Eleanor (1926), "Oration of P.H. Pearse over the Grave of O'Donovan Rossa", in Ead., *A History of Ireland and Her People*, vol. II, London, Phoenix.

HUTTON Brian (2021), "Ballymurphy Massacre Inquest: Coroner's Findings on Victims' Deaths", *The Irish Times*, 11 May, https://www.irishtimes.com/news/crime-and-law/ballymurphy-massacre-inquest-coroner-s-findings-on-victims-deaths-1.4562245 (03/2021).

KENEFICK Michael (2011), "Major Geoffrey Lee Compton-Smith", *Historic Graves,*12 July, https://historicgraves.com/story/major-geoffrey-lee-compton-smith (03/2021).

KISSANE Bill (2005), *The Politics of The Irish Civil War*, Oxford, Oxford UP.

MARTIN Augustine ed. (2011 [1967]), *Exploring English I: An Anthology of Short Stories for Intermediate Certification*, with a foreword by Dermot Bolger, Dublin, Gill Books.

MARTIN S.M. (2017), The Shawlies: *Cork's Women Street Traders and the 'Merchant City' 1901-50*, Dublin, Four Courts Press.

MCCANN Eamon (2006), *The Bloody Sunday Inquiry: The Families Speak Out*, London, Pluto Press.

MCGLINCHEY Marisa (2019), *Unfinished Business: The Politics of 'Dissident' Irish Republicanism*, Manchester, Manchester UP.

MCGREEVY Ronan (2015), "'The Irish Times' Report on O'Donovan Rossa's Funeral in 1915", *The Irish Times*, 31 July, https://www.irishtimes.com/news/ireland/irish-news/the-irish-times-report-on-odonovan-rossa-s-funeral-in-1915-1.2303691 (03/2021).

— (2019), "Marking the Norman Invasion of Ireland: 850 Years and Counting…", *The Irish Times*, 1 May, https://www.irishtimes.com/news/ireland/irish-news/marking-the-norman-invasion-ofireland-850-years-and-counting-1.3877350 (03/2021).

— (2020a), "Historian Finds IRA Commander Tom Barry Tried to Join the British Civil Service", *The Irish Times*, 1 June, https://www.irishtimes.com/news/ireland/irish-news/historian-finds-ira-commander-tom-barry-tried-to-join-british-civil-service-1.4268089 (03/2021).

— (2020b), "Revealed 100 Years on the Letters of a British General Kidnapped by the IRA", *The Irish Times*, 18 June, https://www.irishtimes.com/news/ireland/irish-news/revealed-100-years-on-theletters-of-a-british-general-kidnapped-by-the-ira-1.4281705 (03/2021).

MURPHY Pauline (2020a), "The Amazing Story of General Lucas and His Kidnapping by the IRA", *The Corkman*, 27 June, https://www.independent.ie/regionals/corkman/news/the-amazing-story-ofgeneral-lucas-and-his-kidnapping-by-the-ira-in-cork-39313252.html (03/2021).

— (2020b), "Where did General Lucas go? The Kidnapping of General Cuthbert Lucas", 23 June, https://www.headstuff.org/culture/history/irish-history-history/where-did-general-lucas-go-thekidnapping-of-general-cuthbert-lucas (03/2021).

NATIONAL MUSEUM OF IRELAND, "Historic 'Moon Car' Donated to the National Museum of Ireland", https://www.museum.ie/en-IE/News/Historic-Moon-Car-donated-to-the-National-Museum (03/2021).

NÍ SHÍOCHAIN Saoirse (2018), "The Capture and Death of Major Compton-Smith, 1921", *History Ireland 26*, 5, https://www.historyireland.com/volume-26/the-capture-and-death-of-major-geoffrey-leecompton-smith-1921 (03/2021).

O'CONNOR Frank (1931), *Guests of the Nation*, London, Macmillan.

O'HALPIN Eunan, Ó CORRAIN Daithí. (2020), *The Dead of The Irish Revolution*, New Haven, Yale UP.

O'TOOLE Fintan (2012), "A History of Ireland in a 100 Objects: Pike, 1789", *The Irish Times*, 7 July, https://www.irishtimes.com/culture/art-and-design/a-history-of-ireland-in-100-objectspike-1798-1.531709 (03/2021).

Ó RUAIRC P.O. (2011), "Deserters or Spies", *Irish History Online*, 18 February, https://

www.theirishstory.com/2011/02/18/deserters-or-spies-british-soldiers-execut-ed-at-lough-attorick/ (03/2021).

ROCHE Barry (2015), "O'Donovan Rossa Funeral was 'Rehearsal for the Rising'", *The Irish Times,* 16 July, https://www.irishtimes.com/news/ireland/irish-news/o-don-ovan-rossa-funeral-was-rehearsal-forrising-1.2287409 (03/2021).

RYAN Meda (2012), *Liam Lynch: the Real Chief,* Cork, Mercier Press.

SCALLON D.R. (1999), "A Powerful Political Voice for Catholicism Through Song and Commitment", *Daily Catholic* 10, 152-157.

THE DUBLINERS, "The Merry Ploughboy", https://www.youtube.com/watch?v=VR12Q4kcdqQ (03/2021).

TURNER Martyn, (2002), "An Irishman's Diary", *The Irish Times,* 30 May, https://www.irishtimes.com/opinion/an-irishman-s-diary-1.1058945 (03/2021).

VANCE R.N.C. (1982), "Text and Tradition: Robert Emmet's Speech from the Dock", *Studies: An Irish Quarterly Review* 71, 282, 185–191.

WESTCOTT Kathryn (2013), "What is Stockholm syndrome?", BBC News Magazine, 22 August, https://www.bbc.com/news/magazine-22447726 (03/2021).

WHITE R.W. (1993), Provisional Irish Republicans: An Oral and Interpretive History, Westport, Greenwood Press.

YEATS W.B. (1989), "Easter Rising 1916", in A.N. Jeffares, L.G. Warwick (eds), *Yeats's Poems, ed.* And annotated by A.N. Jeffares, with an appendix by Warwick Gould, London, Macmillan, 287.

Archival Sources

Bᴜʀᴇᴀᴜ ᴏꜰ Mɪʟɪᴛᴀʀʏ Hɪsᴛᴏʀʏ (BMH)

W.S. 1695/ S. 3006, Statement by Witness, Brew Maurice, 1951 https://www.
militaryarchives.ie/collections/online-collections/bureau-of-military-his-
tory-1913-1921/reels/bmh/BMH.WS1695.pdf (03/2021).

API Pᴀʀʟɪᴀᴍᴇɴᴛ UK – HANSARD 1803–2005

Vol 142/ cc1046-7, Common Sitting, Harmood-Banner, 1 June 1921, https://api.
parliament.uk/historic-hansard/commons/1921/jun/01/major-compton-smith
(03/2021).

Vol 131/ cc30-1, Common Sitting, Sir A. Williamson, 28 June 1920, https://api.
parliament.uk/historic-hansard/commons/1920/jun/28/brigadier-general-lucas
(03/2021).

CD booklet cover. Seán Keating, Men of The South (1921–22) © Estate of Seán Keating, IVARO Dublin, 2021. Collection: Crawford Art Gallery, Cork.

Guests of the Nation

by Frank O'Connor

Adapted for Radio by Cónal Creedon.

Guests of the Nation
by Frank O'Connor

Adapted by Cónal Creedon

Produced by Aidan Stanley

Cast

JEREMIAH	Niall Tóibín
WOMAN	Martina Carroll
NOBLE	Liam Heffernan
BONAPARTE	Gary Murphy
HAWKINS	David Coon
BELCHER	Ian Wilde

Commissioned by RTÉ as part of the Frank O'Connor centenary commemorations.

First broadcast by RTÉ Radio 1 on 17th September 2003

Available online: https://www.youtube.com/watch?v=3EjX3Vu6dfY

Intro Music: Extract from Mise Éire by Sean Ó Riada,
    The music should play under the total introduction sound effects
    [Intro Sfx].

Intro Sfx: [Intro Sfx should be extremely brief, offering an audio image
    of rural insurgence during the Irish War of Independence. The
    orchestration of sounds should present a narrative in itself, the
    suggested dialog in the opening sequence is not intended as real
    discernible dialog but rather part of a conglomerate soundscape
    creating an introduction to the events that led to the capture of
    the two British soldiers Hawkins and Belcher.]
    Sequence of sound:
    Voices of indistinct ad lib to be overlayed on sound effects.
    Pastoral, countryside bird sound.
    Trucks arriving from distance.
    General sound of rebels preparing for the ambush. Whispered
    instructions of calm.
    Gunfire of rural roadside ambush reaching crescendo.
    Garbled sound of Irish IRA volunteers frantically talking and
    issuing orders post ambush. Volunteers collecting guns, bullets,
    and equipment etc from dead British soldiers.
    Officers giving orders. Sound of wounded and dying.

    The following exchange should be very short and not performed
    as dialogue, but rather an indistinct sound of voices [cast from
    the play] over general chaos of noise. This should be a full
    ensemble piece of ad lib script offering a general sense of ambush
    chaos and urgency including the implication of two prisoners
    taken.
    – Cease fire! Cease fire!
    Intermittent gun shots.
    [Suggested indistinct text not presented as a radio play, more a
    sense of action in the chaos of sound effects.]
    – There's two live ones here, sir!
    – Come on. Come on. Search 'em.

– What do we do with these two, sir?
– We plug 'em, sir?
– No! No!
– Search 'em.
– One move outa' ye now and …
– Take 'em with us. Get a move on, lads.
– Get them hands up …
– Come on, lads! Come on …
Intermittent gun shots.

Sense of IRA column fading in the distance as they leave the scene of the ambush.

MUSIC: *Fade up music*
Fade down, extract from Mise Éire by Sean Ó Riada.

[Exterior Ambience]

SFX: *Fade up external ambience of pastoral countryside birdsong etc. Fade down slowly under the opening narration by Bonaparte.*

[NOTE]: I suggest to include the random subtle intermittent sound of a crow as an incidental sound effect throughout the play. This will be important and will act as an aural signpost to the end of the play when the sound of disturbed crows punctuates the killings.

BONAPARTE [Narrator]: Funny old thing war all the same.
It's a time when young boys become men and men become boys again.
A bit like …
A bit like a baton in a relay race handed down from generation to generation.
Now, me and Noble? We were that new generation.
And Jeremiah?
Jeremiah O'Donovan was still holding onto his end of the baton with a grip of iron.

SFX: *Cross-fade sound of walking on gravel with intent.*
[suggested] Dog barking. Rural bird song.
Cross-fade intermittent external knocking on a cottage door.

JEREMIAH O'DONOVAN: [Coming on mic] Hello!
Good dog. Good dog.
Hello! Are you there!
You in there! Hello.
Good dog …

SFX: *Sound of door latch and door opening.*
Rural bird song.

WOMAN: [her welcome is more of relief than of surprise] Ah,
Jeremiah …
'Tis yourself.
Come in? Come in …

SFX: General external ambience of door swinging, bird sound maybe
a dog barking.

JEREMIAH: I really haven't time to stop.
Eh? Battalion were on to you? They were?

WOMAN: They were …
… last week.

JEREMIAH: So you know why I'm here …

WOMAN: The prisoners?

JEREMIAH: They'll be moving 'em down here to us tonight …
If that's alright with you?

WOMAN: That'll be fine, Jeremiah.
Fine …

JEREMIAH: Sorry about the short notice …
And the inconvenience. But ehm …

WOMAN: 't is no inconvenience.
… Sur' this house 's always and ever a *safe house.*

JEREMIAH: 't will only be for a week or two.
Three at the most …

WOMAN: [defiant towards the British] You can leave 'em here as long
as you like, Jeremiah.
'til they rot for all I care …

JEREMIAH: I've two young volunteers down at the gate there.
　　　　Noble and Bonaparte.
　　　　They'll be staying with you, just to keep an eye on 'em.
　　　　Are you alright with that?
WOMAN: Fine, Jeremiah.
　　　　Fine …
　　　　[slight change in WOMAN's tone]
　　　　Sur' it'll be a change …
　　　　A bit of company, might be a good thing …
JEREMIAH: Eh? Right then …
　　　　[Shouts] Hoi! Bonaparte! Noble!
　　　　W'ye get up here! Will ye!
　　　　[Quietly to WOMAN] Are you alright?
WOMAN: I'm fine, Jeremiah. Fine.
　　　　[WOMAN regains her composure as the two Volunteers
　　　　approach]
SFX: Approaching footsteps
WOMAN: Two fine looking lads!
JEREMIAH: They're good lads, right enough. Good lads …
SFX: Approaching footsteps.
JEREMIAH: Come on! Come on! Look lively there will ye!
　　　　Noble! Put out that cigarette will ya, for God's sake!
　　　　And stand to attention when I'm talkin' will ye!
SFX: Background sound of NOBLE and BONAPARTE verbal and
　　　　general sound of shuffling.
JEREMIAH: Right lads! Listen to me now.
　　　　When 2nd Battalion get here with the prisoners, for Christ's
　　　　sake look the part will ye!
　　　　They'll be here around 8 o'clock.
　　　　So, keep a light in the window so they'll know the coast is
　　　　clear.
　　　　Have ye got that!
NOBLE: Yes, Jeremiah!
JEREMIAH: Bonaparte?!
BONAPARTE: Eh, right, Jeremiah! Right!

JEREMIAH: In the meantime, secure a place for the prisoners.

WOMAN: I have the room below put aside for 'em …

JEREMIAH: That's great, Missus. Thanks.

But listen lads, make sure the place is secure …

Will ye!

BONAPARTE: They'll be in safe hands with us, Jeremiah.

JEREMIAH: Don't mind your,

[mocking] They'll be in safe hands with us, Jeremiah.

They better be in safe hands!

Because, blast you! If they escape, heads will roll!

D'ya hear me now! Heads will roll!

And look-it, while yer here I don't want ye to be any burden to herself now …

WOMAN: Ah, there's no fear of 'em …

JEREMIAH: Do you hear me?

NOBLE & BONAPARTE: [in unison] Eh, right, Jeremiah! / Yes, Jeremiah!

JEREMIAH: Now, I'll be up a few nights during the week to keep an eye on ye.

So, look sharp! And keep ye're wits about ye!

NOBLE & BONAPARTE: [in unison] Eh, Right, Jeremiah! / Yes, Jeremiah! We will.

WOMAN: Come on.

Come in and keep the cold out…

[Fade scene]

I'll show you where you're bedding down.

This way …

SFX: Sound of door closing.

Cut sound of pastoral bird song

Fade: Sound of walking in house –

general banter of WOMAN welcoming the young volunteers into the house.

NOBLE & BONAPARTE: [in unison fade] Thanks /Right / Thanks very much.

[Scene Sound: Interior Cottage Ambience]

SFX: General interior ambience i.e., intermittent chair being moved, sound of cutlery, fire burning in fireplace.

BONAPARTE [Narrator]: You could cut the tension with a butter knife around the house that day.

And at 8 o'clock sharp, the lads from 2nd Battalion arrived with the two prisoners.

Belcher and Hawkins, their names.

But to me and Noble, names meant nothing.

As far as we were concerned,

They were British soldiers.

They were the enemy.

They were prisoners.

They were our responsibility.

And they'd slit our throats as quick as they'd look at us.

And that's all we needed to know.

Herself served 'em up a plate of poppies and milk.

And she was showing them no favours either …

SFX: General household sound effects – cutlery, saucepans, plates etc.

WOMAN: Ate that there! And be grateful for it!

And if ye think it's a hotel I'm running around here?

Yer in for a bit of a land, me buckos!

BELCHER: Your potatoes are wonderful ma'am …

You grow them yourself?

NOBLE: Hoi, give over your aul guff there, now you!

BELCHER: Bu', bu'…

NOBLE: Shut up yer …

BELCHER: Bu' I was only sayin' …

NOBLE: And I was only sayin' shut up and be quiet!

WOMAN: [Whispering cautiously fearfully to BONAPARTE]

Bonaparte?

Do you think it would be safe to give 'um a knife and fork to ate with?

BONAPARTE: Eh? I'd say, best to give 'um a spoon for tonight. See how we get on.

SFX: Sound of spoons on table.

Sound of plates and delph and kitchen sounds.

BONAPARTE [Narrator]:
That first night me and Noble just stood back watching the two prisoners atein' their supper.

Strange to have the enemy right in the palm of your hand. Totally in your power.

And yet, if the truth be known, me and Noble were scared out of our wits that night.

HAWKINS: Lovely …

Top class grub, Missus. Top class.

BELCHER: Thank you, Ma'am. That was absolutely delicious.

HAWKINS: Wouldn't get the likes of it in the Savoy?

Eh? Belcher?

BELCHER: [Sounds as if he's getting to his feet from the table]

Aye, Not get the likes of it in th' Savoy.

NOBLE: Hoi! Where do you think you're going!

BELCHER: Just thought I'd help Ma'am put the table away …

BONAPARTE: You'll stay right where you are there now, and don't move a muscle 'til I tell you!

D'ya hear me!

Right, Missus, you can clear away the table there …

BELCHER: Bu' all I was doin' was helping Ma'am to …

BONAPARTE: And all I'm doin' is telling you to sit down and stay where you are!

NOBLE: I have 'um covered, Bonaparte.

HAWKINS: [Laughing]

Bonaparte?

You're the bloke they call Bonaparte?

BONAPARTE: And what if I am?

HAWKINS: Just that Mary Brigid O'Connell …

BONAPARTE: Mary O'Connell? What about Mary O'Connell!

NOBLE: Watch him, Bonaparte! Watch him!

HAWKINS: Well, she was askin' about you.

NOBLE: Askin' about me?

HAWKINS: An' sayin' how you had a pair of her brother's socks?

NOBLE: Don't move from that chair now, I'm warning ya!

HAWKINS: [As if pleading his case]

    Madam, while we were guests of the 2nd Battalion …

    met half the bleedin' countryside when we were guests of the 2nd.

    That right, Belcher mate?

BELCHER: [Overlap]

    Aye, met half the countryside …

HAWKINS: We had some right old knees up with the lads over in the 2nd.

    Sing-alongs, dances …

    Tell 'em, Belcher. It's true innit! It's true …

    You and me, mate. With lads of the 2nd.

    Tell 'em, Belcher!

BELCHER: Aye, it's true right enough …

BONAPARTE: Well, you're not with the 2nd now.

HAWKINS: Fair enough, chum. We're not gonna cause you no trouble …

    Are we, mate. Tell 'im, Belcher! Tell 'im …

    Go ask the lads up in the 2nd, they'll set you straight!

    I mean, even if we wanted to run? Where the heck would we run …

NOBLE: There'll be no talk of runnin'! D'ya hear me!

    I'm warning ye …

    Bonaparte, lock 'um up for the night!

HAWKINS: I mean, how far would we get in these khaki uniforms?

BONAPARTE: Right! Ye heard Noble.

    It's lock-up time!

HAWKINS: [Going off mic] Look, mate. All I'm sayin' is …

WOMAN: I'll clear the things off here …

SFX: Sound of cutlery, plates.

NOBLE: Move it. Go on! Get in there!

HAWKINS: Oi! Watch where you're poking that thing, mate?

NOBLE: Go on! Move down to the room! Right quick now!

BELCHER & HAWKINS: [Whispering]
- *You heard him, Hawkins chum!*
- *I don't know …*
- *Just do what he says …*
BONAPARTE: Gowan! Get in there!
Throw us over the aul' padlock there …
SFX: Sound of padlock and chain.
WOMAN: There y'are …
NOBLE: I'll just say this the once and the once only!
Any funny stuff outa' the two of ye and I'll blow the head offa'
yer shoulders!
D'ye hear me! D'ye hear me!
HAWKINS & BELCHER: [agree in unison] Aye – I hear you chum …
NOBLE: I'm not your chum!
BONAPARTE: Double check the aul' padlock there, Noble. Just to be
safe like …
SFX: *[Fade] Sound of hostages and volunteers engaging as they leave
the room.*
Sound of door closing, chains, lock.
BONAPARTE [Narrator]: Sleeping under the one roof with the enemy
is a strange feeling.
So, we never did sleep that first night.
Instead, we stayed up watching the fire burn down.
But as days became weeks,
me and Noble became more familiar with Hawkins and
Belcher.
Got to know their ways like.
I suppose you could say that over the weeks we became like
friends,
except for the minor detail that we were sworn enemies.
'Twas Belcher, the older quieter one that I first warmed to.
Contented old divil. Pure gentleman. Always offering to fetch
and carry for herself.

[Sound Scene: Early Morning Domestic Ambience]

SFX: Maybe sound of cockcrow.
    Sound of door external opening
BELCHER: Only me, Ma'am.
WOMAN: You're up early this morning, Mr. Belcher?
SFX: Sound of buckets rattling.
WOMAN: It's lovely to come down to a lighting fire …
BELCHER: Aye, never one to be loungin' around in the bed, me …
    So, where would you like me to put this, Ma'am?
WOMAN: Show us? You've been down for the water already?
SFX: Sound of bucket on floor.
BELCHER: Aye now, rather down to fetch th'water than sit around
    twiddling my thumbs …
WOMAN: D'y know, Mr. Belcher. You're an answer to a woman's
    prayer. That's what you are.
    You are! An answer to prayer …
BELCHER: Anything else while I'm standing, Ma'am?
WOMAN: [Fade] Well, now that you mention it, Mr. Belcher. There's
    few aul' logs out the back. You'll find the axe in the shed out
    the …
BONAPARTE [Narrator]: … like her shadow he was.
    And she was always flattered by Belcher's attention. A pure
    gentleman.
    Never came across a man so quiet though …
    But his lack of talk was more than made up for by Hawkins.
    Hawkins? Talk for Ireland so he would. Argue black was white
    But he met his match in Noble.
SFX: Fade up card playing scene
HAWKINS: Come on Noble. Queen in to ya …
NOBLE: Ah, eight of trumps …
    What are you talking about, Hawkins?
    Only for the nuns and the brothers and the priests,
    Ireland would have given up all notions of being a republic
    hundreds of years ago.

HAWKINS: Republic!?

> Don't be daft, Noble mate!
>
> Them priests are more Imperialists than bloody well King George himself!
>
> Isn't that right, Belcher! Tell him, Belcher!

BELCHER: All I know, chum – is that it's Bonaparte's deal …

> Give him the deck of cards …

BONAPARTE [Narrator]: Night after night over a hand of cards, same ol' ding-dong.

> Sparks flying between Noble and Hawkins.
>
> Belcher with his long legs stretched into the fire.
>
> Puffin' on his pipe and keeping his hand close to his chest.
>
> And herself?
>
> Herself beaming from ear to ear, just loving the company.
>
> Some evenings Jeremiah O'Donovan would call around and fall in for a hand himself.

HAWKINS: [Fade Up]

> All I'm saying is, if you fellas are sworn enemies of the empire like you says you is?
>
> Well then, what's all this Catholic Church thing all about then?

JEREMIAH: Will ye play the cards! Blast ye!

HAWKINS: You think about it Jeremiah …

> The Catholic Church is the most powerful empire in the world!
>
> You check the map! Just check the map, mate.

NOBLE: I'll tell you straight now, Hawkins boy!

> My brother is a priest. And he's no Imperialist!
>
> Spends his life working for the poor, so he do!
>
> You won't find him lording it around some palace or castle.
>
> Oh no!

HAWKINS: I'm not talking about fellas like your brother, mate?

> No, the priests are only the flamin' foot soldiers!
>
> They're the front-liners like me and you and Belcher and Bonaparte …
>
> They're only out there in the trenches, mate …

BONAPARTE: Here, Jeremiah? Hand us over the cards there and don't
mind those two …
BELCHER: [Whispers to Hawkins]
Yer just digging a hole for yerself, Hawkins chum.
JEREMIAH: Go on, deal the cards, Bonaparte!
SFX: Bonaparte dealing cards. Sound of Bonaparte mumbling as he
shuffles and deals cards.
HAWKINS: Isn't that right, Belcher mate.
It's the cardinals and the pope, They're the flamin' monarchy!
Not fellas like Noble's brother the priest … out there doing the
dirty work for them!
Isn't it true, Belcher! Innit!
WOMAN: Mr. Hawkins! I'll ask you to kindly stop that blasphemous
talk at my table …
HAWKINS: [Sarcastic/ mocking]
Blasphemous talk, Missus?
NOBLE: Now, Hawkins that's you told.
SFX: Sound of general laughter
WOMAN: Who stood up to that bastard Cromwell and his black-
guards only the priests!
NOBLE: Dead right, Missus!
Who fought against William of Orange!
Who were persecuted under the Penal Laws! Huh! Huh!
Only the Catholic priests! That's who!
And where would we be without them?
HAWKINS: That's in the past, Noble mate!
Look!
The way forward is the power of the common man. It will be a
cold day in hell before the common man has the power to vote
in a new pope!
NOBLE: Yeah well, it will be a colder day in hell before we see the
common people of England voting in a new king!
Huh! Huh!
BONAPARTE: Come on, come on …
Hearts are trumps. Play the cards will ye!

HAWKINS: That's what I'm saying …

The Pope and the King of England? Same bloody thing!

JEREMIAH: Would the two of ye just ever give over and play the bloody cards!

You can be dammed sure the Pope and the King have better things to be doing than to be talking about us tonight.

BONAPARTE: Come on, play yer cards will ye …

BELCHER: Three of Hearts played, Jeremiah chum.

SFX: Cards on table.

JEREMIAH: That should draw out a few trumps, lads …

NOBLE: 'tis not the same thing …

How can you say the Pope and the King of England are the same thing!

BONAPARTE: In to you, Noble. Come on, play the bloody cards, will ya …

NOBLE: There!

Bate that!

SFX: Sound of card played down on table.

BONAPARTE: Sho' us?

King of Hearts?!

BELCHER: In to you, Hawkins chum?

HAWKINS: King of Hearts!

You've no scruples about calling on the Royal family when you need 'em,

[Laugh] Hey! Noble mate!

Hey!

BELCHER: Ah, leave it out, Hawkins chum!

HAWKINS: [Fade scene]

All I'm sayin is, it's not like the Pope of Rome or the King of England care a fiddlers for the working man.

BONAPARTE [Narrator]: And that's the way it would go. Night after night.

Sitting around the table playing cards, listening to Hawkins and Noble going at it, knocking sparks off each other …

And, sometimes like a bolt of lightning out of the blue.

Herself would throw in her own two ha'pence worth …

WOMAN: … well, you can talk about empires and the persecution of holy priests and all that.

But look, all I know is that all this upheaval in the world is because of that Italian Count who stole the heathen divinity outa' the temple in Japan.

HAWKINS: The Italian who, Ma'am?

WOMAN: Believe me, Mr. Hawkins. Nothing but sorrow and want and despair follows them that disturbs the hidden powers. Isn't that right, Mr. Belcher?

BELCHER: Never a truer word spoken, Ma'am.

WOMAN: Now, gentlemen …

There's the Queen of Spades!

Follow that if ya can, Mr. Hawkins.

SFX: General sound of comment and dismay and slagging at card played by Woman.

WOMAN: My game I believe …

SFX: General sound of comment and dismay and slagging at card played by WOMAN.

BELCHER: Now, who's for tea?

BONAPARTE: Ah, we'll all have a drop!

NOBLE: May as well make a big pot, Belcher!

JEREMIAH: Count me out, Belcher!

BONAPARTE: You heading off, Jeremiah?

SFX: *Noble & Hawkins:*

[in background continue heated debate until the end of scene and Jeremiah leaves house]

N – you sain' the priests are like us is all wrong …

H – No, no. Yer not listening to me, Noble chum!

N – Not Listening? How could I not listen and you never shutting up!

H – See the Catholic Church and the Royal families of Europe are the same thing …

N – last night you were saying that the priests were communists?

H – No, I was saying a good priest should be a socialist! Not

answerable to the Pope.
N – Communist? Socialist? Same thing, isn't it?
H – Not the same thing ... the Pope in Rome ...
JEREMIAH: Arrah, it's getting late. I should be heading home along.
Good night, lads ...
And thanks for your hospitality, Missus.
I'll be up again during the week.
WOMAN: God bless, Jeremiah!
BONAPARTE: Jeremiah?
JEREMIAH: Bonaparte?
BONAPARTE: Think I'll walk down as far as the gate,
stretch my legs and give my head a break from them two.
SFX: Door open and close.
Cut sound of debate between Noble and Hawkins.

[Sound Scene: Exterior Night Ambience]

SFX: Suggestion: the sound of wind & the odd sound of a crow far away in the distance.
Sound of footsteps on gravel.
BONAPARTE: [light-hearted] That Hawkins fella is some character?
Huh?
Argue with a nun, so he would.
And the other fella? Belcher?
A pure and utter gentleman.
Jeremiah: [Slightly more serious] Maybe you should be heading back up to the house, and eh?
Lock 'em up for the night.
BONAPARTE: [Laughing] Lock 'em up, Jeremiah?
Sur' them fella have no intention of running away.
They're more like guests than prisoners ...
JEREMIAH: [Angry] Prisoners? Hostages!
BONAPARTE: [Still light-hearted] Hostages? Prisoners? Same thing, isn't it?

JEREMIAH: [Furious] Not the same thing!

BONAPARTE: Huh?

JEREMIAH: Look a hostage is a bargaining chip!

They have our lads held prisoner. There's talk of shooting them!

If they shoot ours. We shoot theirs!

It's as simple as that!

BONAPARTE: Shoot Belcher and Hawkins?

JEREMIAH: Dammed Right! Shoot 'em!

And serve 'em right too I'd say!

BONAPARTE: What? Belcher and Hawkins?

JEREMIAH: Listen, Bonaparte. This isn't a game.

We're not playing boy scouts here you know!

This isn't hide and seek!

This is kill or be killed!

Do y'hear me!

Now, go back up and lock 'em in. Like I said!

SFX: Footsteps fade off in the gravel.

BONAPARTE [Narrator]: I watched as Jeremiah O'Donovan disappeared into the darkness

and his footsteps faded to silence.

I stood there, unable to move. Sad. Weighed down.

And later that night, I told Noble what Jeremiah had said.

Noble took it in very quietly.

We agreed it best not to tell Belcher and Hawkins, it would be sort of cruel.

Especially, as it was more than likely that the British wouldn't shoot our lads anyway.

But, by Christ, it was hard to face them next day.

Hard to look them straight in the eye.

Hawkins doing his damnedest to get a rise out of Noble.

But Noble's heart wasn't in it.

[Sound Scene: Internal daytime ambience]

HAWKINS: [Fade up] … the way I sees it, you're as much a

non-believer as I am, Noble mate.

What's heaven? You don't know!

Where's heaven? You don't know!

Who's in heaven? Eh? You know sweet damn all. Do y'mate?

NOBLE: [Not as argumentative as usual] Have it your own way, Hawkins?

HAWKINS: See, y'can't answer!

You know what's wrong with you, mate? You know I'm right! That's what's wrong with you …

SFX: Door opening – Belcher arrives in, sound of carrying wood.

BELCHER: Where would you like me to put the firewood, Ma'am?

WOMAN: Bonaparte, would you get up outa' the fire there and let Mr. Belcher in with the wood.

BONAPARTE: Sorry excuse me …

BELCHER: There we are now …

SFX: Belcher dropping a pile of wood blocks onto the flag floor.

WOMAN: If there were more gentleman like you in this world, Mr. Belcher.

This would be a damn sight better world to live in – and that's no word of a lie.

HAWKINS: You know what, fellas?

Just for a change from the usual game of cards …

I says we organise a bit of a knees-up …

WOMAN: Like a dance? Is it?

HAWKINS: Yeah! Too right, a dance! What d'ya think of that, Ma'am?

Spin 'em around the kitchen and mind the dresser! Wha'?

WOMAN: Oh, mo léir! [laugh]

Wouldn't that be grand!

HAWKINS: The blokes up in the 2nd Battalion used to bring down a fiddle and a drum and a …

BELCHER: It's called a bodhrán, chum …

HAWKINS: Ah, bodhrán? Drum? You know what I mean?

Maybe even an accordion or something?

Invite around a few of the local girls. Dance 'til dawn.

Isn't that right, Belcher mate?

WOMAN: Ah, a dance would be a wonderful thing …

BELCHER: Aye, some wild nights when we were up with the 2nd Battalion.

BONAPARTE: [Abrupt] There'll be no dancing!

Not tonight anyways …

HAWKINS: Belcher here is a dab hand at all your Irish dance steps. Isn't that right?

WOMAN: Do you know the steps, Mr Belcher?

BELCHER: Ah, well, I'm no expert nor anything, Ma'am …

HAWKINS: You name it, old Belcher there has it!

Walls of Limerick. Siege of Athlone. Bridge of …

… naw, I'm wrong there …

Bridge of Athlone. Siege of Ennis?

Lads up in 2nd – said the dances were like a history, isn't that right, Belcher…

BELCHER: Aye, dance steps were how you Irish recorded yer history, innit?

HAWKINS: Now, move that chair, Noble mate. Show 'em, Belcher?

Come on, Noble. Move the chair, mate.

Show 'em, Belcher mate. Show 'em yer steps …

SFX: Furniture moved on floor.

Sound of NOBLE and WOMAN and HAWKINS singing Irish dance tune.

Sound of BELCHER dancing on flag floor.

Sound of HAWKINS' and WOMAN's excited cheering and laughing as they sing tune.

Hand clapping and yahoos of encouragement. Yelps of joy with BELCHER's dancing.

Shouts of, – Good man, Belcher. Etc.

Dancing continues and fun escalates.

Bonaparte suddenly and abruptly stops the merriment.

BONAPARTE: Stop! Stop it!

I said stop it!

There'll be no dancing tonight! Not tonight or any other night!

WOMAN: What's come over you at all, Bonaparte?

You're not yourself at all at all …

HAWKINS: Bonaparte's not himself?

> Look at the face of me old mate Noble there …
>
> He hasn't cracked a smile all day …

BONAPARTE: Shhhh!

NOBLE: Did you hear something?

BONAPARTE: Is that someone down at the gate?

> Stay there I'll have a look …

WOMAN: Probably only Jeremiah O'Donovan up for a game of cards

SFX: Door latch

[Scene Sound: External Night Ambience]

BONAPARTE: That you, Jeremiah?

SFX: Footsteps on gravel coming closer.

BONAPARTE: What do you want?

JEREMIAH: That's an odd greeting, Bonaparte.

> But if you must know I want them two soldier friends of
> yours.

BONAPARTE: Huh?

JEREMIAH: Look before you say anything, there were four of our lads
> taken out this morning.
>
> One of them a boy of sixteen …

BONAPARTE: [Calls for Noble] Noble!

SFX: *Door opening.*
> *External sound throughout the scene.*
> *Every now and again an intermittent sound of a crow in the*
> *distance.*

NOBLE: 'Tis yourself, Jeremiah? Is everything alright?

BONAPARTE: Things don't look good, Noble.

> The two lads …

JEREMIAH: I want you and Noble to bring them out.

> You can tell 'em they're being shifted back up to 2nd Battalion
> or something …
>
> That'd be the quietest way.

NOBLE: No, Jeremiah!

> Leave me out of this…

JEREMIAH: Alright, Noble. You can stay out of it.

    Feeney is with me. He's down by the gate.

    You and him can collect a few tools in the shed.

    And dig a hole down the far end of the bog.

    Meself and Bonaparte will follow you down …

SFX: *[Fade scene]*

    Fade external ambient sound.

BONAPARTE [Narrator]: Jeremiah's voice was cold. So cold and matter-of-fact.

    I could see by the look on Noble's face, what we were about to do had yet to sink in.

    I followed Jeremiah into the cottage.

    Let him do the explaining.

[Sound Scene: Internal Ambience]

JEREMIAH: [Fade up]

    … and that's about the size of it.

    We're bringing ye tonight.

BELCHER: You what, chum?

HAWKINS: You're shifting us back up to 2nd Battalion?

    That's flamin' ridiculous, mate.

WOMAN: For God's sake, Jeremiah.

    Sure, aren't they fine where they are up here with me.

    Sure no one knows they're here …

HAWKINS: Just when a fella makes a home in a place and yer moved on.

JEREMIAH: Orders are orders.

    Get yer coats. We're going now.

WOMAN: There must be something you can do or say, Jeremiah?

    Sur' we're as happy as bugs in a rug here. I'd be lost without them …

HAWKINS: Ah, don't mind about it, Missus. I know how it is.

    When the top brass makes the decisions, 'tis the goons like us has to carry 'em out.

    Isn't that right, Jeremiah mate?

JEREMIAH: … something like that …
SFX: Door latch.
JEREMIAH: Come on. Get a move on.
We've no time for hangin' about …
Right …
SFX: Door opening.
General sound of people moving in a room.
BELCHER: Before we go, Ma'am.
I'd just like to say, a thousand thanks. You're a most welcoming host.
A thousand thanks for everything.
WOMAN: I'll miss ye, so I will.
I'll miss ye around the house …
Miss the company …
HAWKINS: G'bye, Missus.
Thanks for your hospitality.
When this is all over, we might meet again in happier, more peaceful times …
WOMAN: Take care, Mr. Hawkins.
BONAPARTE: Do ye have everything with ye, lads?
JEREMIAH: [Off mic]
Come on so will ye …
SFX: Leaving the house.
BONAPARTE [Narrator]: Without scarcely saying a word we led
Hawkins around the back of the house
and down through the fields towards the bog.

[Sound Scene: External Night Ambience]

SFX: Sound of walking in grass or damp clay.
HAWKINS: Odd, innit?
How come you're bringing us through the fields, mate?
Bonaparte? Jeremiah?
I said, how come yer bringing us through the …
JEREMIAH: [very direct and unwavering]
Four of our lads were shot by your fellas this morning.

We've orders to carry out reprisals.

Sorry to say it. But you two are it!

HAWKINS: Ah now, cut it out, mate. That's not funny.

JEREMIAH: It's no joke!

HAWKINS: That's not funny I said.

You'd put the wind up us with that sorta talk.

So, cut it out.

JEREMIAH: Bonaparte will tell you …

HAWKINS: I don't need to ask, Bonaparte.

Me and Bonaparte are mates.

JEREMIAH: Tell him, Bonaparte …

HAWKINS: Bonaparte?

BONAPARTE: It's true, Hawkins.

HAWKINS: Ah, no? Can't be true?

Christ's sake we're chums, mate.

BONAPARTE: I mean it …

BELCHER: You don't sound like you mean it …

JEREMIAH: Well, if he doesn't mean it? I do!

Now, move on!

HAWKINS: Why the hell, would you want to shoot me, Jeremiah
mate?

JEREMIAH: Yeah, well why would your people want to take out four
of our lads
and shoot them in cold blood!

HAWKINS: That's different, mate.

No, tell us this is all just a big joke …

We're mates for God's sake …

BONAPARTE: There's Noble's lamp over there, Jeremiah.

JEREMIAH: Head towards the light, lads.

HAWKINS: Noble? That you, Noble?

Talk to me, Noble!

I wouldn't shoot you, Noble.

JEREMIAH: You bloody well would!

HAWKINS: He's me mate.

I wouldn't shoot him.

I wouldn't.

He's me mate.

Belcher wouldn't shoot him? Tell him, Belcher.

Tell him!

BELCHER: That's right, chum.

Damned if I would.

HAWKINS: Noble? Answer me.

What do you think I'd do if I were in your place out in the middle of a blasted bog?

What do you think I'd do?

I'd share me last bob with you.

Stick with you through thick and thin, so I would. You know I would …

JEREMIAH: Right enough of this.

Stand where you are, Hawkins.

Don't turn around.

Is there any message you'd want to send before …?

HAWKINS: No there isn't.

JEREMIAH: Do you want to say your prayers …?

HAWKINS: Damn the bloody prayers!

Listen to me, Noble. You and me are chums.

Look, I'll come over to your side.

Give me a rifle and I'll go with you, mate.

Listen to me, lads. I'm finished with all this.

I'm a deserter!

From now on, I'm one of you!

Do you understand!

SFX: Gun being cocked.

JEREMIAH: For the last time.

Do you have any messages to send …?

HAWKINS: Shut up, Donovan!

You don't understand! These fellas do …

We're chums. They stand by me. I stand by them.

We're the same. You and me.

We're …

SFX: Gunshot

> Body falls to ground
>
> Dramatic sound of disturbed crows.

BONAPARTE: Oh Jesus.

JEREMIAH: Right, Belcher …

BELCHER: Don't think Hawkins is quite dead yet, chum.

> better finish him off, mate …

JEREMIAH: Bonaparte, get it over with …

SFX: Gunshot.

> Dramatic sound of disturbed crows.

BELCHER: Poor blighter. Only last night he was all questions about heaven and hell.

> Well, now he'll know as much as he'll ever know.

JEREMIAH: Any last messages, you'd like to send, Belcher?

BELCHER: No, chum…

> Not for me.
>
> But if any of ye would like to write to Hawkins' mum, you'll find a letter from her in his pocket.
>
> My Missus left me eight year ago. Took the kid with her.
>
> Must say, I likes the feeling of home, you might have noticed.
>
> But I doubt I could start all over again though …
>
> I feel, I'm talking a hell of a lot.
>
> It's so silly about me being so handy about the house …
>
> It just came over me all of a sudden like …

JEREMIAH: You don't want to say a prayer?

BELCHER: No, chum.

> I'm ready if you want to get it over with.

JEREMIAH: You understand, Belcher. This is nothing personal.

> We're just doing our duty.

BELCHER: Could never really work out what duty was meself.

> But I think ye're good lads.
>
> If that's what you mean. I'm not complaining

SFX: Gunshot

> Body falls to ground
>
> Dramatic sound of disturbed crows.

BONAPARTE [Narrator]: I don't remember much about the burying,
    only that it was worse than all the rest.
    Back in the house, she was sitting by the fire telling her beads.
    We walked past her into the room.
    She rose quietly and stepped towards to the doorway.
WOMAN: What did ye do with them?
    I heard ye!
BONAPARTE: What did you hear?
WOMAN: I heard ye.
    Do you think I wasn't listening?
    What did ye do with them, Noble?
BONAPARTE [Narrator]: Noble didn't answer her. Then again there
    wasn't a lot to say.
    She fell to her knees and again started telling her beads …
SFX: WOMAN in background praying a decade of the Rosary in Irish.
BONAPARTE [Narrator]: Then Noble went on his knees.
SFX: Noble joins WOMAN in background praying a decade of the
    rosary in Irish.
BONAPARTE [Narrator]: I pushed my way past and stood at the door.
    Watching the stars and listening to the damned shrieking of
    the birds.
    It was as though that patch of bog with the two Englishmen
    stiffening into it was a thousand miles away. Even the
    mumbling of prayers behind me and the shrieking of the birds
    and the bloody stars were all far away.
    And I was very small and very lonely.
    And as God is my judge,
    anything that ever happened me after that I never felt the
    same about again.

Music: Fade Music

Production and cast credits read by continuity.

THE END

The Joy of Writing
after 20 years.

In conversation with Cónal Creedon.

Dr Conci Mazzullo
Università di Catania
concimazzullocm@gmail.com

Biography Note:
Dr Conci Mazzullo holds a PhD in Irish Literature from Trinity College Dublin; the title of her dissertation – *Flann O'Brien's At Swim-Two-Birds and the Construction of an Alternative Heroic Canon. An Intertextual Analysis* (2002). She has published essays and articles on Flann O' Brien and on the Irish sources of his works. She has written a critical study on Cónal Creedon's *Passion Play* (Title: *Station Ireland: Passion Play According to Cónal Creedon*) which was presented at the International Association for The Study of Irish Literatures (IASIL) 2004. She translated *Hofstetter's Serenade* by Eiléan Ní Chuilleanáin into Italian, published in *Studi irlandesi. A Journal of Irish Studies* in 2020. Conci is a photographer and has curated exhibitions in Italy and Nepal. Her most recent publication *Beyond Visible. Parallel Routes Nepal and Italy,* a catalogue of an exhibition at the Nepal Arts Council, Kathmandu, (2018). Conci Mazzullo is an educator, she teaches English and English Literature at Secondary School level, and English and Irish Literature at the University of Catania.

Interview Note:

A strong bond of friendship has been forged between Cónal Creedon and Conci Mazzullo since they first met over twenty years ago. In 2004, Dr Mazzullo wrote a critical study on *Passion Play* (1999), Cónal's first novel. Over the years she has become extremely familiar with his film documentaries and stage plays and is considered an authority on Cónal's wide-ranging body of work.

On the publication of his latest novel, *Begotten Not Made* (2018), it was agreed that she would return to Cork in Spring 2020 to conduct an extensive in-person, walking-the-streets-of-Cork interview with a view to exploring the sense of place in Cónal's work and creative practice. Covid-19 curtailed all international travel, but despite this setback, it was decided to persevere with the interview, which was conducted at a distance between Italy and Ireland. The result is this extremely intimate and comprehensive dialogue which unfolded over a protracted period across various online platforms.

The Joy of Writing after 20 years. In conversation with Cónal Creedon, was first published in *Studi irlandesi. A Journal of Irish Studies* (2020), published by FUP - Firenze University Press. Irishtown Press is very grateful to Professor Fiorenzo Fantaccini for granting us permission to reproduce this abridged version of the interview here in this publication.

Open Access 2.0.

Citation: C. Mazzullo (2020) The Joy of Writing after 20 years. In conversation with Cónal Creedon. Sijis 10: pp. 253-295. http://dx.doi. org/10.13128/SIJIS-2239-3978 – 11769

Copyright: © 2020 C. Mazzullo. This is an open access, peer-reviewed article published by Firenze University Press.

(https:// oajournals.fupress.net/index.php/ bsfm-sijis) and distributed under the terms of the Creative Commons Attribution. Non-Commercial – No derivatives 4.0 International License, which permits use, distribution, and reproduction in any medium, provided the original work is properly cited as specified by the author or licensor, that is not used for commercial purposes and no modifications or adaptations are made.

Data Availability Statement: All relevant data are within the paper and its supporting information files.

Competing Interests: The Author(s) declare(s) no conflict of interest.

The Joy of Writing after 20 years.

In conversation with Cónal Creedon.

Dr Conci Mazzullo
Università di Catania concimazzullocm@gmail.com

Interviewing Cónal Creedon[1] has been a thrilling and intriguing experience, but at the same time demanding. In fact, having known him since 2000 and having shared many and various events connected with *Passion Play*[2] (1999) and the *Second City Trilogy*[3] (2007), it was my intention not to infringe on his privacy.

---

1   This is the link to Cónal Creedon's website illustrating his biography and works http://conalcreedon.com/conal-creedon-biography-books-theatre-tv-documentary-radio.pdf (05/2020).

2   "*Passion Play* is set on Good Friday. It is thematically styled and structured on the gospels of the New Testament. The novel works on various levels. At its most fundamental, *Passion Play* tells the story of a 33-year-old man, whose various paths through life have led him to his current situation – alone, lonely, isolated, living in a kip of a bedsit, facing eviction. With only two hits of LSD and a bottle of whiskey for comfort. His head becomes filled with the sounds of footsteps on the ceiling and a cacophony of voices from another life. Caught in the slipstream of the past, he takes off on a kaleidoscopic odyssey of Marx Brothers' proportions – where the insanity of life is reconciled with the taste of freshly boiled pig's head. In the end, Pluto realises that death is the gateway to eternal life and 'sometimes the need ta die is stronger than the will to live'. *Passion Play* is inspired by two events that have become engrained in the Irish Psyche – the Passion of Jesus and the Easter Rising of 1916. Both events occurred at Easter time and culminate in a blood sacrifice – followed by redemption. The plight of our anti-hero Pluto, reflects the Passion of Jesus and his ultimate ascension into heaven. The recurring theme of Easter 1916 and vignettes from the gospels weave seamlessly in and out of the gritty magic realism of the narrative. Ultimately, Pluto's blood sacrifice leads him to a most beautiful redemption". See Cónal Creedon's website (05/2020).

3   "*Second City Trilogy* was commissioned by the European Capital of Culture 2005. The trilogy is comprised of three short plays: *[The Cure, When I Was God, After Luke]* and is structured is such a way, that the cast of three actors can perform the trilogy in repertory.

From initial reserve, where it felt I was talking more to the writer than to a friend, our dialogue has developed into a freer space and spontaneity. It all started after I went to Cork last Easter and I attended Cónal's reading of *Begotten Not Made*[4] (2018) at Christchurch, Triskel Arts Centre, which sharpened my curiosity to learn about what had led him to write it 20 years after *Passion Play*. In the meantime, I had been pestering him about writing his next novel. So, after the publication of *Begotten Not Made*, we finally got to the interview.

I had planned to meet Cónal at Easter, but Covid-19 made it impossible. We opted to engage online over a protracted period to carry out our project.

CM: As you have published Begotten Not Made, *I thought that I would like to interview you about the novel in this period of lockdown.*

CC: I'd be absolutely delighted; this is such a confusing time. Hopefully we'll all come out the far side intact.

It is conceived as a tragicomic exploration of various father-son relationships, set against the social, historical and topographical background of Cork City. The Second City Trilogy was first performed on 27th June 2005 at the Halfmoon Theatre, Cork Opera House. Due to public demand, the initial proposed production run of two weeks was extended to 6 months – eventually transferring to the main stage of the Cork Opera House. In 2007, the text of *Second City Trilogy* was published by Irishtown Press to celebrate the acquisition by the Crawford Gallery of a portrait of Cónal Creedon by artist Eileen Healy. The portrait features on the cover of the book". See Cónal Creedon's website (05/2020).

4   "*Begotten Not Made*, with illustrations by the author, is a fairy tale for the 21st century, where the mystery of blind faith is explored, and the magic of belief is restored. Brother Scully met Sister Claire only once. It was back in 1970 – the night Dana won the Eurovision Song Contest. Every single morning since their first and only encounter, with a flicker of a light bulb, Sr. Claire has sent a coded message of love to Br. Scully. This Christmas Eve morn, for the first time in almost fifty years, no light shines out from Sr. Claire's bedroom window. And so begins this magical tale of a very real, yet unrealised love". https://dublin-literaryaward.ie/books/begotten-not-made/ (06/2020)

Begotten Not Made was awarded the "Eric Hoffer Award USA", 2020 for Commercial Literary Fiction, and the "Bronze Award for Indie Next Generation Book Award USA", 2020. It was one of five finalists of "The Most thought provoking Book of the Year Montaigne Book Awards USA", 2020 and nominated for the "2020 Dublin International Book Award". It has been cited as "Book of The Year 2020" in the *Irish Examiner,* and "Selection of Top Books of The Year 2019" by Theo Dorgan on "Liveline", RTÉ.

CM: Yes, we'll get through this dystopian story we are living in.

CC: We're telepathic. This very moment I wrote the word *dystopian*. Isn't that bizarre? I've been invited by the Shanghai Writers' Association to include a piece in their next publication, and I was just making a list of words that might work well together, and this very minute I scribbled *dystopian* just as *dystopian* appeared on my computer screen in your message to me – an interesting coincidence.

CM: Let's begin by asking you where you get your inspiration. I would be interested to hear about what inspires you and who inspires you?

CC: I've always been drawn to culture with a small 'c' rather than culture with a capital 'C'. I am fascinated by people I meet. I am intrigued by life as I encounter it. Certainly, at this stage in my life, I could namecheck every inspirational writer, artist and musician, from the classics to the cutting edge and avant-garde, but that would be misleading – that would be superimposing a retrospective inspiration. It would be misleading to attribute my mature life's experience as the inspiration of my immature formative years.

But it is true to say that I have always been inspired by real people in real-life situations rather than literary interpretations or artistic impressions of real life.

CM: Your work seems to focus on Cork City, Ireland, and more specifically on the streets in which you grew up. Could you share with me some aspects of your childhood?

CC: I grew up in what I describe as a *Spaghetti Bowl of Streets* in the North inner city of Cork City. My family has lived on this street for generations, well over a hundred years, back to the time of great – grand-aunt Julia. You know, I am sometimes stopped in my tracks when my nieces and nephews visit the house with their children – it's amazing to realise that on the one hand, those children are visiting their uncle in this very ordinary downtown house on Devonshire

Street – but on the other hand, it also happens to be the house where their great-great-great-grand-aunt Julia lived. That sense of time and space being concertinaed through generations really appeals to me.

We had a shop, a very small shop, the front room of a regular street house had been converted into a shop maybe a hundred and fifty years ago. We weren't wealthy, but we had financial stability of sorts, at a time when many others had nothing.

I grew up surrounded by a big family: 12 children, 2 aunts lived with us on and off and many others who visited and stayed. Seldom a night went by without as many as 20 hearts beating under our roof. Our kitchen was like a cross between a 24-hour canteen and a railway station; there seemed to be people coming and going, and food on the go morning, noon and night. My mother used to say, "It's like Piccadilly Circus".

I was only a kid at the time, and I didn't know that Piccadilly Circus was that massive busy intersection in the centre of London. I assumed she was talking about a circus with clowns, performing animals and acrobats, and that sort of made sense, because there was a circus atmosphere in our house. There was always a sense of free-rolling fun, and you were never quite sure who was staying on any given night.

I was blessed to have eight older sisters and ten aunts. My mother once said that I was five years of age before my feet touched the ground. She was referring to me being held in arms and passed from one sister to another. I believe my personality and perspective has been profoundly shaped by this massive female influence. I sometimes wonder if the gender imbalance of my childhood had been the other way around. More male-orientated than female. I sometimes wonder how I would have turned out had I been born into a family with eight older brothers and ten uncles. I'd probably have ended up in politics or prison or both. [*Laughing*]

My mother had 9 sisters, and my father's brother, Uncle John and Aunt Gretta had 14 children. This meant that there was always a sense of extended family. Consequently, belonging to an extended family

The brothers Con and John Creedon with their wives Siobhán [Blake] and Gretta [White], and twenty-five of their twenty-six children. Twelve children born to Con and Siobhán and fourteen children born to John and Gretta. The author Cónal Creedon is seen here sitting on his father's knee. (Courtesy of Joe Creedon)

or a sense of Clan[5] has always been an important aspect of my life. My father had a very loose sense of kinship, he identified so many non-blood related people as cousins, and all were welcome – but I guess he reserved the title *brother* for one man – his brother John.

Growing up, it seemed as if there was always a sense of occasion in the house regardless of how small the occasion. With so many people living under one roof, every day brought its own celebration: a birthday, a first holy communion, a confirmation, a first girlfriend, a first boyfriend, a first day at school, a first tooth, a first job, a first haircut, a marriage, a birth, or a death.

5   Clan is a word derived from the Gaelic word *Clann*, meaning family group. The Clan system is an ancient Irish / Celtic societal order where individuals identified with a powerful family group, such extended groups are copper fastened through bonds of commerce, protection, property, marriage etc. By nature, a Clan has a strong sense of loyalty to a family name and a very specific geographic location.

CM: Clearly the street on which you grew up had a very big influence and impact on you – I'd like to know more about your life growing up?

CC: Well, I still live on the very same street my family lived and traded on for over a hundred years. It has always been a working-class area. Although I'm not sure the term working class is relevant anymore, it's more a relic of the Industrial Revolution. It represents a caste system that had very little mobility between the classes. As a child, aspects of the 19th Century continued to cast a shadow down our street. Our neighbourhood still had traces of those large multi-occupied houses. Not so much tenements, but large street houses where the tenants lived in bedsits and shared communal landings and outdoor toilets. Lower John Street just around the corner was known locally as Little Baghdad – I assume because of the crowded living conditions and the tradition of hanging laundry across the street. Ours was the sort of place where people socialised on the street, and on summer evenings some would gather around the yellow fluorescent glow of our shop window. Every crossroads, town or village at that time had corner boys, they were our corner boys. I have written about our corner boys in my *Irish Times* column. [6]

Our neighbourhood was a melting-pot of old Cork and those newly arrived to the city. Our shop counter was a meeting place. It was pre-internet, pre-computer – most households didn't have a telephone, and those lucky enough to have television were limited to a single channel, broadcast in black and white a few hours a day. More often than not you'd find yourself staring at a notice on the screen: "Is Dona Linn An Briseadh Seo", which means "We Apologise For The Breakdown".

And late at night, when The Hilton Night Club across the street closed its doors, the musicians from the showbands would gather at our shop counter for a slice of chester cake and a bottle of milk, elbow to elbow with young lovers, off-duty cops, villains and vagabonds,

6   Video Paradiso. Reaching a Turning Point by Cónal Creedon. The Irish Times 27th April 2001.

drunks and bowsies. The Showbands were demigods at the time – Brendan Boyer, Dickie Rock, Joe Mac, Joe Dolan – I guess our shop counter was like a green room for after the gig, before they piled into the van and struck off on the long road home to Waterford, Dublin, Mullingar or wherever they came from.

Pardon me, Conci. But this is a bit of a trip down memory lane for me. You know there were only two late night shops in Cork back then, bizarre when I think about it, our shop and Keane's over on Parnell Place. There was no McDonalds or fast-food joints, people would instinctively make their way to either our shop or Keane's, and, as you'll guess, it was always a fairly eclectic and unpredictable gathering.

Interestingly, our shop would finally shut the door at one-thirty-ish in the morning, and that's often when our house would come alive. Those not yet gone to bed would gather in the kitchen behind the shop and that was often our family time. There were still jobs to be done, such as the newspaper returns and that sort of thing, but without the interruption of the shop being open. When the public aspect of our house became private it was special. The shop would open every day of the year, even if only for just a few hours on Christmas morning – from a very young age I instinctively understood the difference between public and private.

I have memories as a child of my older sisters arriving home from dances with cousins and friends and fun times as the record player would be plugged in. I know dancing in the kitchen sounds like a cliché – but that's the way things were. The shop would reopen again next morning at six a.m. – newspapers for a new day and crates of milk would arrive, and the whole thing would start all over again. It was like the house that never slept.

To this day, I still have the tendency to have two very distinct personalities, the public shop counter me, and the me only those who share my life know. I'm a very different me once I step in out of the street and close the door behind the public shop counter me. I guess there's a certain amount of public persona or performance required when you grow up behind a shop counter. I have described it as *ham acting at the meat slicer.* And maybe that explains why I write. It satisfies the yin and the yang of my personality. The quiet introspective me is satisfied by the process of sitting alone in a room for hours just engaging with the page – probably the time I'm happiest, and the *shop counter me* kicks into action whenever I'm involved in the public presentation or production of my work. Truth be told, I'm happiest alone with my thoughts, but a bit like a shopkeeper, the shop counter is what allows me the space to do my own thing. The social intensity of one allows the social isolation of the other. It is very much a yin and yang existence.

CM: Is it true to say that your work is inspired by growing up in this area?

CC: I guess it's true to say that my Gods have always been local. My heroes ate chester cakes and supped pints of milk at our shop counter. I am inspired by newspaper sellers, fruit vendors, shopkeepers, hawkers, shawlies, pigeon fanciers, dog walkers, republicans, Christian Brothers, villains, vagabonds, heroes, losers, activists, revolutionaries, revisionists, peacekeepers, troublemakers, lawbreakers, lawmakers, prostitutes, nuns, priests, saints and sinners, junkies, alcoholics, vegetarians and vegans.

This is not leafy suburbia. This is where the urban poor collide full on with the merchant princes. The people on both sides of that divide are my neighbours and neighbours become like extended family, I guess you could say a Clan. This is my home and there's no place like it.

CM: And this colourful childhood inspired you to write?

CC: Ah well, it's not as if specific experiences from my childhood inspired my writing. It's not as if there is a box of childhood stories that I dip into for inspiration. It is far more complex than that. It was a headspace, a state of mind, a set of values.

Our shop counter was a focal point for the neighbourhood. My life, my experience, my expression has been informed by the oral tradition of story and song of my childhood, and if that qualifies as inspiration, well, I guess that's where I got my inspiration.

The unfolding life and drama often drifted from the street into our shop and wound its way around our counter right into the little kitchen behind. The neighbours gathered there to entertain and be entertained.

It would be nothing out of the ordinary for a song to break out in our shop – then total silence, as those seated on coal bags and leaning on counters listened intently, hanging on every word of some unfolding epic saga about the day a swan from Carroll's Quay waddled into number 8 down the street just as the cat was having kittens, or how The Scarlet Pimpernel up the street planted the bomb in Coventry and escaped the hangman – reputed to have climbed the prison wall not once but twice. In fact, my mother and father went to visit him when he was incarcerated in Dundrum.

My own personal politics has always been extremely private. We fought long and hard to get the privacy of the ballot box. I find the recent *with-us* or *against-us* culture of social media breeds a society where the voter is a campaigner, and every issue becomes a campaign. The net result is a society that has become totally polarised. It leaves very little room for debate or social engagement.

But if there was a prevailing sense of politics on our street growing up, I guess I might describe it as a blend of trade union and shopkeeper capitalism, dipped in a type of passive Irish Republicanism – very different to the more militant Irish Republicanism found up North. Having said that, three neighbours on our street spent time in prison for their Republican activity – but it's interesting to note that those three individuals would have held allegiance to a very separate and distinct shade of Green.

CM: And has your neighbourhood changed much over the years?

CC: You will laugh when I say that my neighbourhood has changed totally, and my neighbourhood has not changed at all. It is a living entity. Like nature itself, it is never-ending and ever-changing. Our street was predominantly a street of shopkeepers and publicans, and though most shops and pubs stocked more or less the same produce – each shop counter had a specific customer base. An aspect of that customer base was more or less dictated by the place of origin of the shopkeeper. A hundred years ago, all of the shops on our street were run by families who had moved in from various parts of the county. I guess in an Irish context you could say it was an immigrant population, even though the homeplace of origin may have only been 60 miles away. So, for example, our shop, *The Inchigeelagh Dairy*, drew a certain section of customers from Inchigeelagh and Iveleary who had moved from that area to live in the city. This was not some sort of red-necked tribalism or triumphalism, it was more a case of people calling in to get news from home – or, finding a place to stay when newly arrived to the city – or making contacts for work. It could be something as simple as a place where you'd get a lift home on the weekend. But it occurred to me recently that back in the late 1990s, all the small shops on our street had shut their doors and ceased trading, including our family shop. And I remember thinking at the time that it was an end of an era. But I was wrong.

Here we are now, twenty years later, all of the old shops have reopened, and the street is bustling again. The new shopkeepers on our street are Indian, Pakistani, Bangladeshi, Brazilian, Chinese, Russian and Eastern European – the shops are run by families newly arrived to Cork – with a customer base dictated by the place of origin of the proprietors, for much the same reasons as when we were trading on this street. So, as I say, everything has changed and nothing has changed. The big change is that these days I can get a better selection of exotic vegetables and spices.

I always embrace change. And like my father and his father and grand-aunt Julia before him, I continue to engage with the people on my street, those just arrived, and those who have been here for generations.

CM: And what about your teenage years?

CC: When Punk Rock erupted it presented the perfect catalyst for the chemical reaction of youth, mind and energy. Ever since then, I've always been drawn to the true originals: such as John Lydon, Poly Styrene, Ian Dury, John Cooper Clarke and without doubt, Cork's own, Finbarr Donnelly.

The local music scene was bristling with energy, attitude and originality. I was definitely inspired to see schoolmates, banging out originality and doing their own thing on stage in the Arcadia Ballroom, a big old hulking dancehall just down the street from my house, across from the railway station. That's where punk bands gathered in the late 1970s. The message I received was loud and distorted – but clear: whatever I wanted to achieve in life, I would have to do it for myself.

The last job I had, and when I say *job* I mean full-time employment with a wage packet at the end of the week, was with Cork Gas Company back in the early 1980s. And yes, I've had all those other sorts of jobs including building site work, van driving and grass cutting at the Quaker Graveyard, but since the mid 80s, I said goodbye to all that and I've been doing it for myself. I just followed the dream – sometimes the dream can be an absolute nightmare.

This notion of doing it for myself was reinforced by the endless recession of the 1980s: all opportunity just ceased to exist. And without opportunity, you realised you just had to make it up yourself as you went along. I've been more or less making it up as I go along ever since. I wouldn't recommend it as a career path, but it beats working for a living. [Laughing]

My play, *The Cure*, deals with an individual who was so beaten down during the recession of the 80s and was not mentally or educationally equipped to capitalise on the opportunities of our Celtic Tiger economy of the 90s. *After Luke*, another of my plays, also deals with a similar topic – that sense of internal culture clash and inertia during the property boom of the Celtic Tiger. I guess Pluto in my novel *Passion Play* had similar symptoms. He was from the generation of lost opportunity.

CM: So, you have always lived on your street?

CC: By the early 80s, Cork was sinking fast and vanishing down the plughole into the deepest recession. Everyone was leaving for places like Boston, New York, London, Berlin. I went to Canada. At one point, seven of my siblings were in North America and Canada. I stayed there for maybe four years. 1979–1985-ish. I think those years away were so very important.

CM: Why?

CC: First of all, it broke that link with the street at that very pivotal age, in my late teens, when I could have gone down a road that might have brought my life's journey to a very different place. Secondly, being in Canada at such a young age gave me a powerful perspective of Cork as my own place. I believe a writer needs to be slightly removed, and my time abroad gave me that distance. It offered me an objectivity and insight into my own life, an attention to detail of my own sense of place.

When I eventually came home, I saw it for the magical place that it is. My street accommodates everyone from hoteliers to homeless. That's my street. It is a very magical place, maybe not to everyone's taste, but I love it and I live it.

In a way, I find the past a very boring place compared to what is going on in the present. You might enjoy this short piece about my sense of place that was recorded by RTÉ television (CREEDON 2014). There's also a radio interview, ostensibly about my play *The Cure* but it does give an insight to my street (CREEDON 2013).

CM: Did you begin writing when you returned to Cork from Canada?

CC: No. Not at all. When I came home, I opened a launderette right next door to the shop my family traded from. I guess I began writing poems, bits of memoir, unfinished stories in the late 80s while I was working in the launderette. This led to writing radio scripts,

Inchigeelagh Dairy, Devonshire Street, Cork.

and in 1994 I began writing my radio drama series *Under The Goldie Fish*. And very suddenly that became full-time. I was producing a half hour of radio drama every single week. I think we made eight series in total between 1994 and 1998. I was writing frenetically, and with a deadline of a half hour of drama every week, I learned the ability to write anywhere. At the time I had an old Volvo parked outside the launderette – that's where I sat and did most of my writing, it was comfortable, warm but above all it gave me privacy while continuing to work in the launderette.

I still have reams of handwritten scripts from that time. Around that time my short stories started to gain a bit of recognition: the George A Birmingham Award, Francis McManus Awards (RTÉ), PJ O'Connor Awards (RTÉ), BBC One Voice Monologue Award and The Irish Examiner Life Extra Award.

Back in the 1980s/90s, people/artists/friends from flats and bedsits around would drop in to my launderette for the company. It was the sort of place where people could hang out, smoke cigarettes, talk.

I was certainly influenced by the artists and art students hanging out in my launderette. Even though working in the launderette was humdrum, and not an easy way to earn a living, by the early 90s it became a bit of a hub where a lot of young people hung out. I guess in those pre-internet, pre-mobile phone, pre-social media days – people relied on actually meeting people, so maybe identifiable places to hang out were treasured. A place where you instinctively knew there would be people to engage with, and I guess my launderette was one of those places. We'd often regroup back to the launderette after the pubs. I had a cassette player there. Had some fairly raucous, late-night 'poetry readings'. Must be one of the few launderettes in the world that was raided by the police to break up a rowdy 'poetry reading'. It would be nice to say we talked about art, but no – in truth, I was in my 20s and it was a rolling party: art exhibitions, book launches, poetry readings and the associated table of free wine – were just seen as the kick-off to a good party. At one point the launderette doubled as a little local micro home brewery – the heat from the dryers made it a perfect place for fermentation. Laughing here, remembering a crateload of bottles with the caps exploding off – beer everywhere – literally, the place smelt like a brewery.

Reminds me of my first book launch, Pancho And Lefty Ride Out (1995) which was held down the street in Murphy's Brewery – absolutely coined the phrase, *piss-up in a brewery*, that night. It was fairly insane. Well, what would you expect in a free bar in a brewery during a recession?

Unemployment was so high in Cork that for the want of something to do, everyone seemed to be a musician or an artist. Art was at the centre of everything. And the realisation that self-expression could be considered as work was a huge eye-opener for me.

My house became an open house. I would say there are probably close to 20 artists and stall owners and shopkeepers around the town now, who lived in my house at one time or another between the years

1988 to 1999. My house was very much a come-and-stay sort of place. The living conditions weren't great; electric cables running all over the place and no proper heating, water taps not working, rattling windows, leaking roof, all that sort of thing, but that's the sort of house it was. It was a big downtown, rattling, leaky old house. Back then the bedsits were often in a worse condition – Pluto in *Passion Play*[7] lived in a bedsit house. Comparatively, my place was more comfortable. I had space and there was always a party.

Even to this present day my house is still very much an open house. Located downtown, it's the sort of place where people drop in to chat, some stay. Some evenings I cook for guests, even though I may not have invited anyone, people just seem to turn up.

CM: Getting back to your inspiration, clearly your narrative is inspired by the streets on which you live, but how about the influence of other artists?

CC: With regard to other writers and artists? Well, I'm totally impressed by human endeavour and am very lucky to have met so many of my heroes and found them to be just as impressive in real life. But when it boils down to it, I'm impressed by people and how they interact with people – and I'm entertained by art.

Truthfully, I'm inspired by the private person more than the public aspect of their work. So, in the context of art and literature, I'm inspired by the artist not the art. I am inspired by people from all walks of life, and more often than not I find inspiration from outside the arts community – but if you are asking specifically about artists? Many of the artists who really inspired me you may not have heard of – people such as Ciarán Langford, Kevin Holland, Eilís Ní Fhaoláin, Chris Samuels, Alice Maher, Finbarr Donnelly, Ben Reilly, Helen Farrell, Dimitri Broe, Suzy O'Mullane, Paddy Galvin, Desmond O'Grady, Theo Dorgan, Maud Cotter, James Scanlon, Sean McCarthy, John Spillane, Martin Wedge, Martin Finnin, Irene Murphy, Mick

7   Passion Play (1999), a novel by Cónal Creedon.

O'Shea, Maurice Desmond, Tom Campbell, Harry Moore, Eileen Healy and so many others – it's a list that continues to grow right to the present day – the art scene is so vibrant, it's like swimming around in an ocean of inspiration.

Back in the 80s/early 90s, a group of maybe twenty or more artists moved into a big old semi-derelict warehouse at the end of my street – they called themselves *The Backwater Artists*. Their arrival into my neighbourhood became a massive turning point in my life.

It was like the changing of the guard. All the old families had moved out. I deal with that subject matter in my first short story, *After The Ball* – where once I had countless friends while growing up living on these streets – just like that, they were all gone. But then the Backwater Artists moved in and it was like having a ready-made group of friends living at the end of the street, same age, same concerns, same interests, same neighbourhood. It was such a perfect stroke of luck.

That generation of artists opened my eyes to the fact that self-expression could be a way of life. I'm ever grateful that I was inspired by those artists to follow my dream and eventually I found the courage to close my launderette. It was a bit like jumping from an airplane without a parachute – but hey, sometimes you just gotta grab life and give it a squeeze. The Backwater Artists Group has gone from strength to strength and is now located in a new state-of-the-art centre of workshops, galleries, print facilities on the Southside. And though I'm not a visual artist, thirty years has passed, and I still consider myself to be one of The Backwater Artists and thankfully, they still invite me along to openings and parties. Life can sometimes deal a funny hand of cards – well, the day The Backwater Artists Group moved into my street it was like getting four aces and a joker up my sleeve.

But for the most part, the people who inspired me and my work don't work in the arts at all. In order of importance, I would list Fiona O'Toole – after thirty years, nobody knows me better than Fiona knows me – I would go so far as to say that Fiona knows me better than I know myself. Next in order of inspirational importance would be my parents, then my uncle Jack and auntie Kit, after that it spreads out to my siblings, extended family, friends and neighbours and that hierarchy of inspiration has remained more or less intact over the decades.

CM: Well, as you said I don't know those artists. I know that Patrick Galvin wrote poetry?

CC: Ah well in fairness, I wouldn't expect you to know the people who inspired me, inspiration is a very private experience, a very personal exchange. At every pivotal point in my life, I have been blessed that there were always certain individuals standing in the wings offering encouragement and lifting my spirits. Paddy Galvin was one of those people at a very specific time in my life. Life is long and my friendship with Paddy blossomed within a very specific short window of opportunity, and I'm glad that destiny gave me the opportunity to know Paddy.

CM: When did you meet Patrick Galvin?

CC: It seems like Paddy has always been connected to my adult life, so I really have no idea how we met.

Obviously, there was a generation of age between us, but we enjoyed each other's company. Our connection was not based on his writing or my writing, we were just good friends, nothing academic about it. We had a lot in common. We laughed a lot. As you may know, Paddy grew up on Margaret Street in the south inner city, which is almost identical to my neighbourhood on the north inner city. Neither of us had attended UCC, but both of us were appointed Writer-in-residence at UCC – incidentally both of us were also writers-in-residence in Cork Prison. We both toured America as guests of The Irish American Cultural Institute. We ploughed a similar furrow, we both found our inspiration in the streets, we were both multi-disciplinary, we both wrote novels, stage plays, poetry, film scripts, radio plays. Paddy composed and recorded songs, and lately, I too have drifted into working with musicians such as Claire Sands and John

Spillane (SANDS 2019; SPILLANE, CREEDON 2020). More recently with orchestral composer John O'Brien and the Cork Opera House Orchestra, DJs Fish Go Deep, Shane Johnson and Greg D, and sound artists Mick O'Shea, Harry Moore and Irene Murphy. I guess Paddy Galvin and I shared the view that it's all about engaging with life and people – stretching the elastic until it either snaps or springs back in your face. [Laughs]

I often performed with Paddy for visiting groups. He was a very humble man and such great company. I remember, I think it was Christmas 1996, Paddy asked me to meet him at the Quay Co-op. And eventually, he took two sheets of paper out of his little bag. He had handwritten two versions of *The Mad Woman Of Cork*. One was presented on the page like a standard poem, the other had the stanzas scattered all over the page. He asked me which one I thought was best? I said, in my opinion the one that was all over the place was the nicest. And with that, he tore up the version that was like a standard poem and handed me the copy that was all over the page. – "There, that's for you for Christmas", he said.

Seemingly, I had mentioned to him that I liked that poem. Although, I think my favourite poem by Paddy is *Plaisir d'amour*.

I was also very fond of his wife, Mary Johnson and their daughter Grainne and son Macdara. Of course, there was the added connection of the Spanish Civil War. Paddy and Mary had a big interest in the Spanish Civil War, and my father's cousin, Mick Riordan, was one of the last surviving members of the Connolly Column who went to fight the fascists in Spain. As you probably know, the Spanish Civil War manifested itself like a Civil War in Ireland, where the Irish Blue Shirts supported by the Catholic Church, went to fight for Franco, while the International Brigade fought against Franco.

My father's cousin, Mick Riordan, had been prominent in the IRA and went on to set up the Communist Party in Ireland. He was ultimately excommunicated by the Catholic Church – which made life extremely difficult for him and his family back in the days of holy Catholic Ireland – when the Catholic Church ruled the roost.

But in later life, as the cosy cartel of church and state lost its grip, and Ireland became more secular, Mick Riordan was accepted back into Irish life. There were a number of Spanish Civil War celebrations and of course Paddy and Mary would always come along and play a very active part.

Actually Conci, I introduced you to Mick Riordan, that day you, Piera and I went to Dublin maybe twenty years ago. Mick used to run the Communist/Socialist bookshop in Temple Bar, Connolly Books. I think you may have bought books there that day we visited, perhaps a copy of his book *The Connolly Column*?

(*And here Cónal Creedon shares a link to a song* (MOORE 2011), Viva la V Brigada *by Christy Moore – inspired by, Michael Riordan*)

Christy Moore wrote this song. He says he was inspired to write *Viva la V Brigada* following a meeting with Mick Riordan. Before Mick died, Christy Moore came along to sing it at his bedside.

Mick Riordan grew up around the corner from our house on Pope's Quay, near the Dominican Priory, that's sort of ironic considering his relationship with the church. Mick worked in the buses with my father, and the Riordan's also had a shop – on Adelaide Street – called the Ballingeary Stores, reflecting their original home village. Ballingeary is the neighbouring village to my father's home village of Inchigeelagh – so there was always that overlap of family connection. I am very close friends with Mick's son and daughter Manus, and Brenda. There's something about those generational links that is so profoundly solid yet impossible to quantify.

CM: *It's interesting that your cousin was excommunicated by the Catholic Church. You seem to write a lot about religion, particularly in* Begotten Not Made. *Were your parents very religious people?*

CC: Well, I suppose before I begin talking about my family it would be important to say that even though each individual member of my family lived a shared experience – each individual experience would have been very different.

For example, my oldest sister was born into the austerity soon after World War II. She entered this world an only child, with all the

Cónal Creedon on the street where he lives. © Michael McSweeney

attention of a firstborn. Her father was in his twenties, married to the most beautiful young love of his life. My sister's parents were a young couple who had just moved to the big city. They were starting out on life having taken over a busy shop from grand-aunt Julia. His life was full of dreams, ambitions and hopes for the future.

Whereas I was born into the swinging 60s, my father and mother had twelve children, my father was well into his forties, my parents were tired, approaching late middle-age – their dreams and ambitions for the future were very much a thing of the past. So, within the same family, within the same individuals, the differences of expectation, experience, perspective and memory will be vast. So, I am very conscious of the fact that I'm not a spokesperson for my family's experience – each individual experience is unique and bespoke.

But, in answer to your question, in my experience, no we wouldn't have been a particularly religious family. Culturally we were Catholic.

ART IMITATING LIFE IMITATING DEATH

And back then Ireland was extremely Catholic, but as a family we only engaged with religion as an extension of our culture and our history, rather than any sense of blind religious devotion. So, like everyone else we took the Catholic sacraments: baptism, holy communion, confession, confirmation, marriage.

I don't have a memory of our family going to Mass as a family unit, not even at Christmas or other church holidays. So, no, we weren't what one would describe as a devout family. Having said that, like every other Irish family, I had a number of cousins attached to various religious orders. Clerics – priests and nuns were regular visitors to our house, but their visits were secular and social, not religious. The bishop of Cork has been a lifelong and regular visitor to our house, ever since he was a student in the seminary in the late 1950s. He came from Inchigeelagh, the same village as my father. My mother and father became like surrogate parents to him here in the city. Though retired now, he is 80, he is still considered extended family.

So, *Begotten Not Made* is obviously influenced by my many and varied interactions with the Catholic Church, clerics and religion in general. *Begotten Not Made* is about a seismic shift that happened in Ireland sometime around the end of the 1960s. Dana winning the Eurovision identifies the moment when everything changed, and the island of Ireland ceased to be insular. Ireland was ready to step forward and join Europe as an equal. Meanwhile, Brother Scully viewing the rising sun as the *Changing of the Guard*, identifies the time when the old guard of the Catholic Church became redundant as keepers of Irish morality.

If one looks at the numbers of new vocations to the Catholic Church – right up to the late 60s young people were still flocking to join religious orders. Brother Scully was one of that last generation. By 1970 it had stopped. Vocations stopped suddenly like a tap being turned off.

Begotten Not Made, is set against the last generational wave of young Irish people who flocked to join religious orders, and then suddenly they were left high and dry by an Irish culture that had moved on.

I have visited our local monastery and there are no young brothers there at all, just a handful of very elderly brothers, and there's something sad about that.[8] When I was a kid that monastery was like a beehive, full of fit, sporting young men who held huge influence in this city. The North Monastery school was a massive institution in what would have been considered a deprived working-class area. These were not the children of captains of industry or merchant princes – but the Brothers prepared generations of boys to feed directly into significant aspects of Irish life: sport, culture, politics, civil service and semi-state bodies. There was a sense that the brothers had real influence in various aspects of administrative life. The power behind the powerhouse driving the country – The North Monastery became a seat of power.

I often think those elderly clerics must feel short-changed by the way current Irish culture has forgotten them, life in Ireland has changed so dramatically around them. And that is really what the book is about. It's about how our *belief* – not just religious belief, but our cultural belief changed dramatically at that moment in time.

In *Begotten Not Made*, I consciously stayed away from the many scandals that have rocked the Church: sex abuse, mother and baby homes, etc. – that would have been another book, another story. Obviously, it's all in there, bubbling under the surface, but in a very peripheral way. That aspect of holy Catholic Ireland is well referenced in the narrative, but this novel is not about that. *Begotten Not Made,* is very much the view of the world from inside the head of one man. This is a specific story about a young man who realises he is devoting his life to a great lie, but due to the entrenched cultural morality of the time, he is unable to do anything about it. Like a lobster pot, there's no way back out. The tragedy is, when the cracks became apparent, he finds himself trapped on the wrong side of a shift in culture.

8   The Christian Brothers set up in Cork in 1811, when Brother Jerome O'Connor and Brother John Baptist Leonard set up a small school for young boys in and around the impoverished lanes of the Shandon area of the city. The last of the Christian Brothers left the North Monastery School without pomp or ceremony during Covid epidemic in 2021.

CM: *Your previous novel* Passion Play *was published twenty years ago in 1999. When did you first think of* Begotten Not Made? *While you were assembling* Passion Play? *Or just after it?*

CC: I think I may have first told you about *Begotten Not Made* back in the early 2000s. Basically, *Passion Play* is set on Good Friday with many biblical references and a strong Jesus theme running through it. Then I wrote the play *The Prodigal Man,* commissioned by RTÉ Radio (2001), which was a reworking of the Prodigal Son parable, that brought me back to the bible and Christian thinking again. I had written two other stage plays, *When I Was God* (1999), followed by *The Trial of Jesus* (2000) which was a re-enactment of the crucifix-ion of Jesus. A site-specific play, performed on the streets of Cork on Good Friday 2000, two thousand years since Jesus' death, it was part of the Irish National Millennium celebrations.

I plunged deep into biblical research for *The Trial of Jesus,* and I think it may have occurred to me at that time that there was a strong case to be made for King Herod as Jesus' father. In 2001, I had a weekly column in *The Irish Times* – Video Paradiso. It was a fiction-alised account of my life centring around watching a film every week. I laugh when I see the column title, Video Paradiso – it was so long ago the DVD had yet to be invented. Online streaming? YouTube? Box sets? I may as well be saying, – "Beam me up, Scotty!" [*Laughing*].

Well, that Easter in my column, I wrote about the biblical film, *The Greatest Story Ever Told* (1965), and I put out the theory of Herod as Jesus' father. I imagined a situation where Jesus was standing in front of Herod Antipas, beaten, scarred and dressed in the faux crown and Herod mockingly bowing down before him saying – "Hail King of the Jews!" And then it crossed my mind, maybe Jesus did have a claim to the throne, maybe Antipas and Jesus were half-brothers? What if Antipas and Jesus were both aware that they were half-brothers and this day of reckoning had been written in the stars since the arrival of the *Three Wise Men* kicked off the *Slaughter of the Innocents*? I then backtracked both of their stories through the scripture, and it seemed to be a narrative that actually held water.

It just so happened that *The Irish Times* decided to defer my column for a week. And so, the following week Easter had passed, and that particular seasonal film had lost its currency, so the piece with my theory on the paternity of Jesus was not published – and I wrote a different piece about a different film for the following week. So my theory about Herod being Jesus' father did not appear in print. Maybe the editor wasn't comfortable with where that column was going. That was the only week the column was deferred – maybe it was just coincidence.

I had begun working on the novel *Glory Be To The Father*. It had fatherhood as a main theme, so I decided I'd weave the theory about Herod as Jesus' father into the novel. I had great plans to finish the novel that year, but then as often happens, my writing took a different direction. I started writing stage plays and radio drama. I think *Glory Be To The Father* will be my next book. We'll see. [9]

CM: What did you write next?

CC: I had written a mountain of radio plays throughout the 90's – maybe forty or fifty hours of radio drama, so I continued writing radio plays in the early 2000s – *Caught in A Trap, The Battle of Kinsale 1601, Guests of the Nation, The Tailor and Ansty* – for RTÉ. *This Old Man* represented Ireland in the World Play Awards and was broadcast on networks across the world, and *No.1, Devonshire Street* was commissioned by BBC Radio 4 and BBC World Service. I then wrote five stage plays between 2000 and 2005: *Trial of Jesus, Glory Be To The Father, The Cure, When I Was God, After Luke.*

Somewhere between 2005 and 2009 I made five film documentaries, *The Burning of Cork, Why The Guns Remained Silent in Rebel*

---

9   Since this interview was published, Cónal's writing has taken a diversion. In 2021 his collection of short stories, *Pancho And Lefty Ride Again*, has been published – awarded One City One Book and is one of five finalists in the Next Generation Book Awards 2022 USA. *Art Imitating Life Imitating Death, an Exploration of Guests of the Nation by Frank O'Connor*, will also be published later in 2022. Conal intends to publish *Glory Be To The Father* in 2024.

Cork, Flynnie, The Man Who Walked Like Shakespeare, If It's Spiced Beef It Must Be Christmas and *The Boys of Fair Hill*. The documentaries are inspired by aspects of life in my own neighbourhood. I guess you could say the documentaries are an extension of my writing.

Then between 2009 and 2015 I began touring my stage plays abroad. In 2007 Fiona O'Toole and I set up Irishtown Press/Productions specifically to tour my plays internationally. We published the scripts of my plays, as a calling card that could double as a programme for our touring productions. We were surprised to find that there was interest and a demand for publishing my work. So, Irishtown Press became more active. We published *Passion Play, Begotten Not Made, Pancho And Lefty Ride Again* and republished an updated version of *Second City Trilogy*.

In those ten years, I had a total of maybe six tours to China and six productions of my plays in New York, picking up awards for Best Actor, Best Director and Nomination for Best Playwright at the First Irish New York Theatre Awards. Our productions received high acclaim in the New York Times and That's Shanghai – so it's really been a great experience. Seat of the pants sort of stuff – but what's life about if it's not about taking chances. We've made some very special lifelong friendships through those collaborations, Hu Peihua at the Shanghai Writers' Association in China and of course Michael Mellamphy, Ciarán O›Reilly and Charlotte Moore at the Irish Repertory in New York and Elizabeth Osta among others stand out.

I was commissioned to write the book, *The Immortal Deed of Michael O'Leary*, published in November 2015 to coincide with the centenary of *World War I*. In the context of everything I've produced or written, that book is unintentionally a most personal and detailed exploration of my own childhood. It tells the true story of Michael O'Leary, a man from my father's home village, Inchigeelagh. A man who has been totally airbrushed from history due to an unfortunate twist of fate. It's a fascinating story.

Meanwhile, all the time since 1999, I had been writing my current work in progress, *Glory Be To The Father,* which included *Begotten Not Made* as a sub-strand narrative. Along the way I busied myself doing other bits and pieces, writing radio plays, reading tours, and taking on roles such as Writer-in-residence at UCC. That brings me exactly to where I am right now: just about to pull together and finish my next novel, *Glory Be To The Father.* The beauty of my life is that I never know what I will be doing any given week. I basically wake up each morning and follow my heart. Projects that may have been sitting dormant on a back burner for decades can suddenly just leap to the top of the queue – so it's never a dull moment.

CM: Can you tell me about your fascinating experience as Writer-in-residence at UCC?

CC: My appointment as Writer-in-residence at UCC came just at a right time.

The previous 10 years had been bananas. Making film documentaries and touring to USA and China with plays and screenings of my documentaries. It was like bang, bang, bang – and I was fortunate to have been invited to present several reading tours in Europe, China and the USA. The Irish American Cultural Institute invited me to do a whistle-stop, seven-city coast-to-coast tour of America. That decade was extremely full-on. It was a hectic decade but it was such great fun.

So, in 2016, when I was appointed Writer-in Residence UCC, it was a privilege to be able to weigh anchor for a year and focus on what I was doing in UCC. Initially, I was concerned that I might not rise to the challenge, as I had not attended UCC as a student. I had very seldom ventured inside the gates of UCC. Interestingly enough, as someone who prides myself in being very engaged with the city, UCC was a strand of Cork life I knew nothing about.

But from the first day I arrived at UCC, I knew I had landed on my feet. I loved the luxury and the privilege of having work colleagues. My role was twofold. Firstly, to set up and teach a module for MA students, and secondly, to engage with the student body in general.

During my first week in UCC, I put the word out that I wished to be involved in a writers' workshop, and so it began. From day one, I insisted that we were all writers, I wasn't a teacher. Our room was always an open forum, and we talked a lot about everything and anything and nothing at all, most of all we laughed a lot. I guess I just wanted to soak up the whole essence of campus life, so I engaged with students from the various societies and departments across campus, German, Italian, History, Music, Theatre, Digital Humanities …

You'll laugh, but true to form, I regularly led the students on walks around the town instead of being tied to a classroom. It was great to just wander around, everyone throwing in their tuppence worth, talking about details of architecture, street features, shopkeepers, history, geography, myths, stories, folklore and a whole host of characters we'd meet on our travels around the town. They were an extremely bright and engaged group. I found it to be such an inspiring and invigorating time. It was during my time as Writer-in-residence at UCC that I finally began putting *Begotten Not Made* together.

Even though that was 6 years ago, I'm still in contact with the students, staff and faculty, and was so honoured to be appointed Adjunct Professor of Creative Writing. I really don't have an ambition to be a teacher, it is a huge responsibility, and I don't think I'd ever be able to take on such a serious responsibility over a protracted period. I guess it's like the difference between being a parent or a fun uncle/ aunt. I'm happiest standing in the wings, and, if every now and again I can help by offering a little levity and encouragement, that is perfect.

CM: So, your time in UCC as Writer-in-residence gave you the time to finally finish Begotten Not Made.

CC: Yes, I was given time by the very fact that I had a regular income. But more importantly, I was given the inspiration and the encouragement by the students. It was a highly charged and creative environment.

CM: Where did you get the idea of Jesus as the son of Herod?

CC: As I mentioned earlier, between 1997 and 2001 I had become immersed in a number of bible-inspired projects and the idea just occurred to me. The theory of Herod as the father of Jesus is all in the interpretation. Brother Scully's deconstruction of the gospels in *Begotten Not Made* totally demystifies any ambiguity, and makes a very strong case for the thesis that Herod the Great was Jesus' father.

That aside, there are many theories regarding the paternity of Jesus. I'm fascinated by the fact that the most popular theory is also the most farfetched and unlikely. The most popular obviously attaches him to a deity or a God, while other theories are more secular, including the Roman soldier Tiberius Julius Abdela Panthera[10], who was supposed to have had an affair with Mary, as the Greek Philosopher Celsus reports, and of course there has always been a finger of suspicion pointing at Joseph himself as the father. But the detail of who the father was or wasn't is unimportant. What matters is that a young Christian Brother became so consumed by his faith, that his obsession with *belief* effectively destroyed his vocation and ultimately his life.

CM: But is Begotten Not Made *a story centred on faith and hypocrisy in monasteries and convents in Cork?*

CC: Monastic life in this novel is simply presented as another aspect of life. Life within a monastic setting is no more hypocritical than any other slice of life, with its internal jealousies, greed, power struggles, ambitions, loves and heartbreaks. The Christian belief is just the backdrop from which a religious community operates. I guess the real thesis of *Begotten Not Made* is: if we scratch the surface of any fundamental belief system, religious or secular, we may find that the very basic cornerstone belief is not as solid as it appears to be. The survival of such a community depends on the core belief remaining intact,

---

10 "In the 2nd century, Celsus a Greek philosopher declared that Jesus's father was Panthera, a Roman soldier. But Origen, who considered he was referring to a fake story, replied: "Let us return, however, to the words put into the mouth of the Jew, where 'the mother of Jesus' is described as having been 'turned out by the carpenter who was betrothed to her, as she had been convicted of adultery and had a child by a certain soldier named Panthera". (Origen 1980, 3).

Artists outside Backwater Art Studio Pine Street Art Trail 1997.

unchallenged, entrenched and in the realm of the unproven. Belief only works if people can be convinced that such a belief is a special magical mystery of life and remains beyond question.

CM: How did you develop the idea of belief throughout the novel?

CC: Attempting to reveal the true fundamentals of any organisation or social communal gathering can reveal more complicating questions than definitive answers. In short, the whole book is about belief. Herod as father of Jesus is a smokescreen from which I present and explore a plethora of other belief stories within the narrative.

A measure of good fiction is the ability to stretch the limits of plausibility to the limits of credibility. The core of this novel is effectively about two extremely unlikely unrequited love stories that develop within enclosed religious settings – the lifelong love affairs between Brother Scully and Sister Claire, and the apparent lifelong love that is shared by Sister Francesca and Mossie the Gardener.

By including several incredible stories in the narrative, it makes the surreal love stories at the core more acceptable. By questioning the fundamental belief of Christianity – Jesus the son of God in heaven, born of a virgin, crucified and raised from the dead – this in some way, makes all the other fairy tales in the narrative – heroic pigeons, flashing lights, saintly apparitions, miraculous cures – seem more plausible.

In the context of *Begotten Not Made,* by holding the big belief, the paternity of Jesus, up to scrutiny it allowed me to tell what I believe to be the real story of the book, a very magical fairy tale of two unrequited love stories of four individuals trapped in religious life. Two love stories trapped by belief.

CM: Beyond the 'belief stories' explored in the narrative, did you wish to highlight the process of secularization in monasteries and convents in Cork?

CC: Yes. But not so much to highlight it, I am more interested in identifying this huge cultural shift that happened in my lifetime. The last time you were in Cork we went to the Nano Nagle Centre, housed in the renovated 18th-century South Presentation Convent.

Well, Nano Nagle is in the process of being conferred to sainthood, meanwhile the convent she set up is in the process of being secularized. Ironically, this is basically the backbone of one of the primary narratives in *Begotten Not Made*, the beatification of Sister Francesca of the Birds at a time when St. Joseph's convent is in decline.

When I was writing *Begotten Not Made* back in 1999, I could not have anticipated or even envisioned such a thing would really happen at South Presentation Convent. A short twenty years ago, it would have been unheard of, that such a prestigious Catholic Convent would be repurposed as a public space, rebranded as an arts centre/café, public gardens. Even the nuns' chapel is now a concert venue. Up until recently, this community of religious Sisters lived behind large stone walls, but now the walls are removed. It has become a place where tourists go for a coffee and can lounge around taking the sun in what used to be the nuns' private garden. The nuns are more or less all gone now from South Presentation Convent.

In *Begotten Not Made*, Reverend Mother has a vision of these changes ahead, she is somewhat cynical about it – but she is also a realist, the convent is in decline, she views this redevelopment, repurposing of the convent as an opportunity – and needs must (see Creedon 2018, 299).

The Ireland I grew up in was extremely Catholic, I'm sure your experience in Italy was similar. The Mass was presented in Latin, reading the Bible was not encouraged. It was this ownership of the 'belief' that gave these men of the Church so much power, and of course by the time I was growing up in the early 70s all that was about to change dramatically. The world I knew, and my parents knew had changed, and changed forever.

CM: Was Brother Scully's hysterical laughter a way to show his / your disillusion with the triviality of certain miracles which served Christianity to attract 'primitive minds', as you say in Begotten Not Made?

CC: No. His hysterical laughter is far less contrived than a response to the incredulity of the miracles. Basically, Brother Scully is an emotional mess. His manic laughter is a symptom of his mental instability, partly because of the cocktail of heavy medication and treatment he has received over the previous 50 years. (SEE CREEDON 2018, 166) He has learned that laughter is more socially acceptable than crying, so all his emotions are expressed through laughter. Brother Scully's laughter is psychologically deep-rooted, it is in fact an expression of his isolation, his loneliness and emotional disconnect.

CM: While rereading it I felt that the text moves through different blocks that could be seen as different 'short stories'. The first one about Brother Scully's 'doubts' about Christian dogmas with the theory of Jesus, son of Herod. The second about the so-called miracles told by the 2nd narrator, Sister Claire, stories within stories …

CC: Oh yes, that? If I presented the theory of the paternity of Jesus in one block it would read like an academic thesis. It would be extremely information-heavy with facts and chronological dates and an endless cast of key individuals to be introduced as characters. It would not read like fiction. It would require the full backstory and exposition of secondary biblical characters – John the Baptist, Elizabeth, Zacharias, and the various members of the Herod Royal family – also an analysis of the political situation that was unfolding in Jerusalem at that time, including the workings of Roman rule and methods of maintaining law and order in Judea.

I decided it would be better to present the story three times. By doing this, the reader becomes complicit in the conspiracy that is unfolding in Brother Scully's mind. The first telling is a very simplistic naive exploration by Brother Scully while in the seminary, when he questions the Theology Master, Brother Ambrose, about details of scriptures and, in the process, exposes some minor anomalies in the biblical story. In doing this I establish the main players of the story that is about to unfold in the minds of the readers and put forward the idea that there are narrative flaws in the New Testament.

Once the reader is familiar with the main characters, the goodies and the baddies established, the story is told a second time. This time Brother Scully expands his theory to Sister Claire. This second retelling presents the bible story, personalities and characters as a real flesh and blood family, the saga unfolds like a soap opera.

The third bite of the cherry is at the end when Brother Scully has a late-night discussion with Brother Ambrose. This intense scrutiny of the theory informs the reader that there is, in fact, a good solid scriptural basis behind the theory of Jesus' paternity.

It would not have been possible to present this intense debate without having first informed the reader of the historical context and background, and the personalities, the frailties and fallibilities of the key characters.

CM: And you introduce stories within the stories, is this the device you use to lighten the narration? Was the theory of Jesus' paternity meant to be structurally framed by the different narrative blocks of stories within stories?

CC: This is a book of stories. Multiple interlocking stories untangle inside one man's tormented mind over one day. The basis of all good storytelling is to convince your audience to suspend disbelief. I use the various fairy tales within the narrative – heroic pigeons, love stories, saintly apparitions, miraculous cures – to give space to the reader to become comfortable with the challenges of the biblical and theological narrative. And conversely, I use the biblical exploration as a grounding counterbalance to the fairy tale aspect of the other stories.

There's also a certain type of repetition in each retelling. This gives the reader ownership of the theory rather than presenting it as a long list of facts. It was important for me that the reader would engage with Jesus' extended family as a real-life family with its own internal conflicts, struggles and complications in a narrative storyline rather than present it as an academic theological theory.

CM: Your books and plays regularly feature the characters going for a walk around the city of Cork, Do Pluto's walks in Passion Play *cover a similar route in* The Cure *and in* Begotten Not Made?

CC: [*Laughing here*] You'll find I do bring my characters on walks around the town all the time, or maybe it's the case that my characters bring me on walks around the town. Going for a walk around town is one of my own personal, favourite past times. To tell you the truth, I enjoy bringing my characters and my readers for a walk. It gets me away from my desk without leaving my desk.

My walks usually take a very specific route in my head, but the details on the page never exactly fit any map. In *The Cure* there are two walks. One walk is very specific and unchanging. It is the walk taken by the protagonist's father and grandfather so many times that he can mentally namecheck every scent along the way – he literally conducts this walk with his eyes shut. From the grotto in Blackpool all the way to my street, including namechecking the shop in which I grew up on Devonshire Street. This walk is revisited four times in the text, and it can appear like a druidic chant, getting faster and faster and less descriptive as we get closer to the end of his journey: Patrick's Bridge, the gateway to the downtown.

Meanwhile there is also a second walk in *The Cure*, the protagonist in real-time is also walking through the streets of Cork in search of an early morning pub. It's Christmastime, and on his journey, he meets his past. These encounters with his past force him to re-examine the present.

You might find it interesting that his issues with the Church become somewhat resolved after he steps into a church on French Church Street. Of course, if you examine a real map, you'll find there is no church on French Church Street – it's a name that goes back to the Huguenots' arrival to the city. Meanwhile, the protagonist is attempting to get to an early morning pub on Fr. Matthew Quay for a drink – known in Cork as *the cure*. I guess Cork people would instinctively know that Fr. Matthew is the apostle of temperance, so heading to Fr. Matthew Quay for a cure (a drink), may imply that alcohol will not be the cure. And of course, Fr. Matthew Quay? Of the many quays in Cork, Fr. Matthew Quay is the one if not only quay that does not have pub. Here's a guy who is struggling with alcohol and he is heading to a quay dedicated to the Apostle of Temperance, seeking an early morning drink on a quay that does not, in real life, have a pub. It's in the title. He's looking for a cure [11] and ultimately, he finds a cure, but the cure is not found in a glass.

So, yes, I bring my readers for a walk, but the street map I'm using does not exist. It is informed by a deeper layer of what it means to be *of Cork*, rather than *about Cork*. I'm inclined to play with the city and its make-up, its history, culture, myth and legend – and that informs the parameters of my fiction.

---

11   A Cure is a slang term in Cork, that describes an alcoholic's early morning drink. That first drink of the day is known as 'a cure'. It enables the alcoholic to face a new day. In fact it's not a cure, but rather it prolongs the illness of alcoholism.

Meanwhile, the walks in *Passion Play* are of a different nature. The first one begins outside the Donkey's Ears pub when Pluto meets the young Mags, and he takes the drug Ecstasy for the first time. It is fuelled by the drug which has the effect of spiralling energy and Pluto gets extremely talkative which ends in an explosion of sex with Mags. This walk begins on the Southside by City Hall and follows the river, circumnavigating the *old town* and eventually he finds himself in the heart of the Northside at Shandon steeple. Along the journey, some of the episodes he talks about are tinged with autobiographical and historical detail. You might find it interesting that Pluto, though wired on drugs, when they get to Dalton's Avenue on the Coal Quay, he makes the comment that there should be a bridge built across the river there. The book was published in 1999, and many years later Cork City Council actually built a bridge at that very spot on the river. You'll laugh, but leading directly to the front door of my father's cousin – Mick Riordan's house.

Pluto's second walk is fuelled by LSD. At this point in the novel, he is dead, and his soul takes off in a chaotic, multi-episodic, trippy, frantic walk. Due to the LSD influence he gets side-tracked by a pigeon in the river, then there's the toilet bowel episode, then the DVD to be returned, then he meets Tony Tabs. It's a rolling snowball of a journey – obviously the energy is driven by the LSD, but what you might find interesting is that both walks in *Passion Play* end up bringing him to the Shandon area, *Under the Goldie Fish*[12].

In the first walk he ends up having mad, wild passionate sex with Mags in Shandon graveyard. In the second walk he's back in the Shandon area for his son Paulo's holy communion. Incidentally, Paulo was conceived during a sex session in Shandon graveyard during the previous Ecstasy-fuelled first walk with Mags.

The novel ends with a walk up Patrick's Hill, and Pluto finds himself in Bell's Field, spellbound looking at the grand vista of the Northside. It dawns on him that the Northside, 'the city of pain', is

12 Under The Goldie Fish, is the name of Cónal Creedon's extensive radio drama which ran for eighty half hour episodes over four years. RTE 1994 – 1998.

actually his vision of heaven. This vision of heaven, as described in the final chapter has remained relatively unchanged since it was captured in Butt's famous landscape of the 1750s.

There are several walks in *Begotten Not Made.* When Brother Scully goes for a walk on the beam of light across the sky from Monastery to Convent, this is obviously a virtual walk where the young Brother's demented mind presents him with an overview, a grand vista of the world he left behind, the world outside the monastery wall. Some of the people mentioned are real people, familiar on the Northside of Cork City: Michael Crane and Gerry Dalton are both well known in the pigeon fancier fraternity of the city.

Another walk in *Begotten Not Made,* is when the word filters out of the Convent that Sr. Francesca cured a pigeon – that news is carried in a very specific journey. Beginning in the heart of the Northside in Jack Forde's pub in Shandon, down to the North Gate Bridge, along the North Main Street and South Main Street. Then filtering out across the island of downtown Cork, and over the South Gate Bridge up into the heart of the Southside and into the snug of Tom Barry's pub in the heart of the Southside. This is specifically written to display what I describe as the *butterfly wings* nature of Cork city.

Bringing my characters on a walk is very much part of establishing the world of the book, or the play, in my head. Similarly, in my play, *After Luke,* the journey from the yard down to the bingo hall is very much mapped out and repeated again and again to include the detail of the 'speed bumps' as a metaphor for the narrative of the play itself. And though audiences and readers might recognise the walks, and some might even believe they have walked those walks, the fact of the matter is that the walks are not precise topographical maps. So, the walks are mental and emotional walks. I don't want to be trapped by the exactness of the detail of a map. At the end of the day, it is a world of make-believe which offers a mirror to reality.

CM: I've been rereading Brother Scully's confession and it sounds like the Inquisition Trial of people already found terribly guilty who had to admit that Satan misguided them!

CC: Well, first of all it wasn't a confession as such. It was a trial conducted by Deputy Head Brother Lynch and Bossman. Christian Brothers don't have the authority to hear confession, only priests are qualified to hear confession. And that explains why, later that night when Bossman slept soundly, he had a very vivid and surreal dream about the bishop coming to him to tell his confession. It's a power game to have the authority to hear a confession. It puts man the confessor in the position of God the Creator.

The whole notion of Satan is introduced by Bossman seeking cheap thrills. He wanted to hear about the young nun's body and the sexual details of the act that occurred between young Brother Scully and Sister Claire. So, he introduced the notion of confession and Satan and the temptation of Adam by Eve to legitimize his probing questions about the sexual act. There is a sense in the text that Bossman becomes more and more sexually aroused by the details, which ultimately leads to sexual orgasm. Where he sits in the darkness and lights a cigarette in the calmness is very much a post-coital scene.

CM: Why was confession so intimidating when you generally know the penance was three Hail Marys?

CC: Confession! Don't start me on confession! The basic premise of confession is that we are all guilty of something. Even before birth we are guilty of Original Sin – save me please! Personally, confession is one of my biggest issues with the Catholic Religion. Basically, when I was a child Cork was predominantly a Catholic city.

I find the fact that every man, woman and child went to their local parish church to tell another man, albeit a 'man of God', exactly what they had done 'wrong' is a total abuse of power. The KGB, the Stasi or Maoist China did not have such a network of compliant information gathering from the general population that the Catholic Church had.

The secrecy of the confessional also creates the perfect 'safe' environment for devout individuals to reveal information about their neighbours, employers, their families, etc. Basically, the Church

Cónal Creedon with UCC student writers' group.

through the system of confession gained insight into every single household right across the country. It also elevates the priests, these pampered men, to a position of almost demigod in the community. Personally, I find it infuriating when I think of my mother's generation, morally devout women of her time – going on their knees, with their heads covered, in a darkened confession box to confess their 'sins' to some fucking eejit of a priest – pardon my English. Even the notion of men entering a church bare-headed, while bishops and cardinals parade around the altar wearing the most outrageous headgear is elitist and fundamentally unchristian.

So, to be clear, the penance wasn't the problem – the process was the problem. I remember when I was a kid, it crossed my mind that it didn't matter if you committed murder or robbed a penny lollypop, the penance would always be the same: Three Hail Marys. So, even back then I felt the whole idea of repenting and absolution of sins was just a smokescreen for information gathering. If the local priests know who is robbing from their bosses, who is having an extra-marital affair, or involved in other more 'devious ungodly' practices such as homosexuality, or involved in illegal organisations etc., and this information can be gathered and cross-referenced through 'confession', that gives that organisation a frightening amount of power over the weakest, most vulnerable individuals of society. Yes, I think confession is so frighteningly insidious, particularly when you had kids as young as 7 years of age inside in a darkened confessional sharing their innermost thoughts and experiences with a strange man who claims to be in regular communication with the God of Creation. Frightening! Jesus save us! I agree with most of Jesus Christ's message, but I don't see Christianity in any of that.

CM: Brother Scully's spontaneity and belief in Bossman's line of enquiry entrapped him inside a net of hypocritical behaviour condemning him before even starting to listen to his confession. As you say, "Frighteningly insidious"! Did you have any personal experience which led you to refuse confession and what you rightly thought the morally wrong listening to people's weak sides of their souls?

CC: Confession was certainly the first of the sacraments I rejected. I'd say I was maybe 9 or 10 years of age. At a very young age we instinctively knew it was a load of rubbish. I remember as kids, at the end of our confession we used to tag on one extra sin: "…and I told lies, Father".

By doing this it exonerated us from telling the truth to the priest in confession. For example, you could make up a few innocent sins, such as "I didn't do my homework, I didn't bring the dog for a walk…" and leave out the more serious sins. And if at the end of your confession you just say "…and I told lies, Father". In that way you were confessing that the confession you had just told was a pack of lies. I'm laughing here, but we had this figured out at 10 years of age.

I remember not having been to confession for several years – for some reason, I found myself in a confession box with a priest at the far side of the grill. I would guess it was around the time of my Confirmation. At the part when the priest invited me to say the Confiteor. I just couldn't remember the words of the prayer. It had been so long since my previous confession, for the life of me, I just couldn't remember the words of the prayer. All I could do was to repeat the opening words again and again, "Oh, my God ... Oh, my God... Oh, my God..." and I remember thinking this is ridiculous and farcical – and truthfully it was frightening.

Eventually the priest recited the prayer line for line, and I repeated it back to him, and even at that young age I realized this is just a load of aul' rubbish. I do believe that was my last time going to confession. As you know Frank O'Connor wrote a very famous short story, *First Confession*, set in my local parish church. Well, maybe I should write a sequel: *Last Confession* [*Laughing here*].

CM: I think that in Italy, after the II Vatican Council, things started to be more lenient. We were much freer than in other countries where the Catholics had to prove their fidelity to the Catholic religion.

CC: Absolutely, Vatican II was the beginning of the end, but I think Pope John had seen the writing on the wall and was trying to steer the church towards a modern age. But that goes back to what I was saying at the beginning of this interview. In any belief system, the fundamentals cannot be questioned. By attempting to modernise the belief system, Pope John may have inadvertently undermined the belief.

Certainly, an Irish Catholic is not the same as a Roman Catholic. Devout Irish Catholics are very connected to local pre-Christian deities. Irish Catholicism has been integral to the 800 years of struggle against the oppression of our English colonists. I don't mean Irish Catholic as a type of ritualistic practice but more as a cultural identification tag.

Simply put, the line of demarcation would be: 90% of the population, the 'native' Irish, were Catholic, meanwhile a small minority constituted the ruling class – the English invaders/colonialists were 'Anglican/Protestant'. Ever since Henry V111 in the 1530s, and more particularly after the Desmond Wars of 1570's, this Catholic/Protestant divide always caused a certain amount of conflicting issues regarding indigenous Irish spiritual belief and political aspirations. And certainly, Catholicism was the flag of the Irish rebel.

The 1798 Rebellion complicates this broad stroke theory as many leading protestants were the leaders of the United Irishmen. But for the most part, the Catholic Church was at the head and the centre of how 'native' Irish culture was expressed and defined. That is probably the main reason why Irish Catholicism became the state religion. Catholicism was handed the responsibility for Irish morality, education and health since the War of Independence 1921. It also explains the culture that allowed, if not actively enabled, so many recent scandals – sexual scandals, mother and baby homes, the abuse of power in education, and so many other aspects of Irish life.

In the context of the novel, *Begotten Not Made* – in very simplistic terms, the arrival of television offered the ordinary people of Ireland a more global view – the Eurovision Song Contest is pivotal to the liberation of Brother Scully. In *Begotten Not Made*, you may remember arch-conservative, Deputy Head Brother Lynch's, stark warning that television would be the end of Catholic control in Ireland (SEE CREEDON 2018, 58). Television, as he saw it, the great educator of the masses, was in fact the Antichrist.

CM: In Italy we were very lucky, because my generation attended higher secondary school after 1968; this meant we were much freer than the previous generation which had gone through World War II. Young people radically contested political, social, cultural, economic structures, refused capitalism through the students' movement in Europe and USA and somehow, then, culturally influenced society.

CC: Well, very similarly Ireland went under dramatic change from late 1960s through the 1970s, and that's the backbone of *Begotten Not Made*. Deputy Head Brother Lynch in one of his rants gives out about students rioting across Europe in 1968 (SEE CREEDON 2018, 58).

CM: What about Brother Ambrose, who was gay, why did he commit suicide? While talking to Brother Scully he finally emerged as a free-thinking man who knew things as they were and appeared easy-going and critical of the Brothers' system.

CC: Brother Ambrose explains why he took his own life. Basically, it was the realisation that the Christian God was a God of conditional love that pushed him over the edge. I'm not even sure if Ambrose would have classified himself as 'gay', he knew he was attracted to young males, but may not have fully understood that this was the 'mortal sin of homosexuality'. His sexuality was a complication for him. I believe he struggled with his feelings and may not have fully understood them. Of course, there is a massive contradiction and irony in Brother Ambrose – he is a theologian – and yet his sexual orientation would suggest that he would refute the sexual rules imposed by Church Theology. And, as a Theology Master his role was to encourage younger Brothers when they were experiencing conflicts of faith, meanwhile his obvious sexual orientation meant he was continually in conflict with his own faith. There is also something interesting in that – his role in the monastery places him in charge of the young, idealistic, newly-arrived seminarians. Was this a role he manipulated for himself? As Deputy Head Brother pointed out very early in the book – was the whole religious community functioning in a state of denial?

If Brother Ambrose had been a younger man he would have left the monastery, but as an older man, his options were limited. He was trapped, nowhere to go. His only way out was to take his own life rather than live a life of hypocrisy.

It's important to remember that Ambrose had recently been accused of having late-night sexual encounters with the young seminarian Brother Crowley, so realistically, his secret life within the monastery had been exposed, his suicide may have had more to do with that, and very little to do with his conversation with Brother Scully.

CM: *So how were you inspired for Brother Scully's love for the novice (Sister Claire)? Did you know of Brothers and Sisters who took their lives?*

CC: I don't know of any Brothers or nuns who took their own life. But back then suicide was a mortal sin, pardon the unintended pun. So, a death by suicide would not be generally reported, talked about or admitted.

Regarding clerics falling in love and leaving a religious order, I am aware of many. I'm not sure which came first, the inspiration or the experience. A Christian Brother from our school left the monastery and married a nun. A number of years ago, long after I had written the bulk of this book, I arranged to meet him, not so much to find out about leaving the monastery, but to learn details of day-to-day life as it unfolded inside a monastery.

For example, I asked him how they would address the Head Brother, would they call him Head Brother? And he laughed and said: "No, we used to call him something like the Bossman". In a way, such a simple answer was a breakthrough moment for me. It really opened my mind to the notion that religious orders were just a functioning community within the community.

Another was a young priest. I went to London with my father back in the early 1970s. We stayed in this young priest's flat – it was a shock to me at the time when I realized that he was married to a nun. And even though I was only a kid at the time, there was a sense that I shouldn't talk about it when we returned to Ireland.

But there are many, many cases of young lads of my vintage who went off to join religious orders, many of whom quit and ended up getting married and having kids.

The big change of the 1970s was the ability to reject the church and its power – and continue a secular life – that would have been far more difficult, if not near impossible, for an earlier generation.

CM: Did you give importance to all the names chosen for your characters as I presume you chose Scully coming from the Irish Ó Scolaidhe?

CC: I picked Scully for many reasons. His name changed many times over many drafts, but I stuck with Scully, because it sounded like *skull* which gives a sense of foreboding – and the whole narrative happens inside his skull. Well obviously, Scully would have connotations of 'Scoil', the Irish word for 'school'.

Here's something that might interest you, Conci. Br. Crowley in *Begotten Not Made* is actually Fatfuka in *Passion Play*. Fatfuka, the missing years. [*Laughing*]

In *Passion Play*, Fatfuka went to join the Christian Brothers and left under a cloud. You might remember he had a brief gay affair with Pinko before he married his wife and had children, and then of course he got cancer and died.

Well, Brother Crowley offers a glimpse into what had happened to Fatfuka while he was in the Brothers. It's implied in *Begotten Not Made* that Br. Crowley and Brother Ambrose may have had a brief relationship before Br. Crowley walked out of the Monastery.

Meanwhile Christy, the child in *Begotten Not Made*, is the protagonist in my next book, *Glory Be To The Father*.

CM: So, we have got characters moving inside your macro text, interestingly, from Passion Play *to* Begotten.

CC: ... and further afield, some of them will move on into *Glory Be To The Father*. Yes, like Mossie the Gardener also turns up in my next book as a pivotal character. But they're not put in there as an act of continuity on my part. In fact, readers would really have to know my work very well to realise it's the same character from a previous book. Often the name changes – for example Brother Crowley is never referred to as Fatfuka in *Begotten Not Made*. Having said that, we know in *Passion Pay* that Fatfuka's surname is Crowley, but he is never addressed as Crowley – so it's there if one wants to find it, but it's not important. And Mossie the Gardener from *Begotten Not Made* is known simply as Grandda, in *Glory Be To The Father*. I suppose it's really me just enjoying my own writing process, and engaging with characters that are very much alive in my head, rather than attempting to be clever.

CM: Getting back to Begotten Not Made, *I wonder could Brother Scully see the Southside of Cork, i.e., the Nano Nagle Centre from his window?*

CC: I believe you might be getting two Presentation Convents confused. Nano Nagle is a former Presentation Convent located on the Southside of the city; in fact, it's located just around the corner from Margaret Street where Paddy Galvin grew up. But North Presentation Convent is another convent run by the same Presentation Order of nuns but located on the Northside.

Brother Scully is in a monastery on the Northside of the city. In real terms he wouldn't be able to see a convent on the Southside of the city. But, having said that, it's best not to be bogged down in the detail of topography. Brother Scully's world is not necessarily identified as Cork. Cork as a location is not mentioned anywhere in the text. So, it would be very misleading to identify what he can or can't see in Cork city. So, even though the book is immersed in Cork, the topography is imaginary and intentionally not detailed enough to identify what he can or can't see. Although, in my mind's eye, Brother Scully is on the Northside and the monastery would be the North Monastery. And Sister Claire's convent would be North Presentation Convent, which is adjacent to the North Monastery, but I don't reference them by name. Yet many of the references are very much Northside: Murphy's Brewery, the stacks of houses of Goldsmiths, Rathmore and Audley Place, Patrick's Hill, Shandon, and of course the pigeon fanciers named in the book. Michael Crane and Gerry Dalton are real Northside Cork people.

Whereas the Nano Nagle Centre is very much on the Southside of the city, but it is fascinating that the recent repurposing and proposal of sainthood for Nano Nagle is a mirror of what is happening in the fictional convent in *Begotten Not Made*.

CM: But what was the Nano Nagle area like in the 50s? Always the Northside against the Southside? Was it the same in the 1950s-70's?

CC: Cork City Northside and Southside are carbon copy images of each other. In the past, the old walled city of Cork was located on an island in the middle of the river Lee. The English colonists restricted indigenous native Irish access to the old city of Cork. This old walled city is still identifiable to Cork people as the warren of streets between the North Gate Bridge and the South Gate Bridge. The Gate Bridges were in place to keep the native Irish out. Over time, two separate communities of indigenous native Irish established themselves either side of the river, separated by the old walled city, an island in the middle of the river. The Northsiders and the Southsiders view each other from opposing hillsides, but for generations had very little social contact or interaction. This is what I describe as the *butterfly wings*.

If you fold the map of Cork using Washington Street as the axis – which bisects the old city – well, all those buildings and industries and streets on both sides of the river align almost perfectly. Yet both communities were separated and isolated by this 'old walled town' in the centre of the river.

Shandon steeple on the Northside reflects the tower on Tower Street over on the Southside; the North Cathedral reflects the South Cathedral; the North Monastery Christian Brothers reflects the South Monastery Christian Brothers; the Northside Presentation Convent reflects the Southside 'Nano Nagle' Presentation Convent; the Northside Murphy's Brewery is reflected by the Southside Beamish Brewery; the Northside O'Connor's Funeral Home is reflected by the Southside Forde's Funeral Home. Even the streetscape, the hill of Shandon Street is reflected by the hill of Barrack Street, and the respective offshoots of Blarney Street and Evergreen Street are almost identical.

I believe it is this separation and yet similarity of two communities that has nurtured what was traditionally such an entrenched and sometimes bitter Northside/Southside rivalry in Cork, a rivalry probably not so evident in recent years.

That sense of the Northside and the Southside being carbon copies of each other is identified in *Begotten Not Made* (see CREEDON 2018, 189-190). I describe the opposing hills of the Northside and the Southside as the *butterfly wings* in the passage where Mossie the Gardener gossips about Sister Francesca's miracle in a pub on the Northside, and the news travels from one pub, *Jack Forde's*, *The Shandon Arms* in the Shandon area on the Northside to the corresponding pub, *Tom Barry's*, in Greenmount area on the Southside:

> — *It's a miracle, whispered Mossie the Gardener.*
> *No, not a miracle, said Sister Francesca.*
> *She was annoyed that Mossie would suggest that God the Father, creator of heaven and earth, would concern himself with something as trivial as curing a small bird's broken wing. She was adamant that no miracle had been procured and insisted that the bird's recovery had been nothing more than a combination of care and the power of prayer.*
> *Gardening can be thirsty work, and sometimes gardeners drink more than they should. That evening on his way home from work, young Mossie the Gardener dropped into the Shandon Arms for a pint or two. Word of the robin's miraculous recovery spread along the bar counter like ink on a blotter, through the snug, past the card players in the corner and out into the lanes around Dominick Street and Eason's Hill, then right across the city from the northern tip to the southern tip of the butterfly wings, from the laneways at the top of Shandon Street, all the way down into the bowels of the town, across two rivers, past mirror images of breweries, bridges and undertakers. Then shopkeepers and shawlies contrived to whisper and gossip from the North Gate Bridge, the full length of the North Main Street, and down along the South Main Street, all the way to the South Gate Bridge. The word travelled cheek by jowl up the steep climb of Barrack Street and swept into the maze of little houses that is Greenmount. Later that evening, when Johnny the Echo boy poked his head into Tom Barry's snug and said,*
> *— Ladies? Did ye hear about the young nun up in the Northside?*
> *The news was there before him. They turned from their jugs and spoke as one.*
> *— About the miracle, is it?* (CREEDON 2018, 68).

The irony of the piece is that the news travelled from North to South before the newspaper man arrived with the evening newspaper.

Indicating that these two separate and isolated working-class communities were totally in sync and almost subversively connected to each other.

Incidentally, Johnny the Echo boy is a real person, he has sold *The Echo* newspaper on the streets for decades. Johnny Kelleher (RIP), I dedicate a nod of recognition to him in *Passion Play*. Johnny Kelleher is remembered in Cork for his agility, ducking and diving like a dancer between the traffic at rush hour outside the Colosseum on MacCurtain Street. I am fascinated by the idea of a street newspaper vendor carrying spoken news as well as print media news.

CM: As for the story within the story, i.e., the miracle of St. Joseph, did you hear about anything similar, visions among nuns in your "extended neighbourhood"?

CC: There are/were so many whisperings of spiritual events in Ireland. Our Lady appearing in Ireland became a huge phenomenon back in the mid 1980s, 35 years ago. It all began in Cork, in a place called Ballinspittle. Within weeks the phenomenon was reported to be happening in shrines up and down the country, including in my father's home village of Inchigeelagh. This wasn't a case of one or two children seeing an apparition of the Blessed Virgin, I'm talking about literally tens of thousands of people witnessing what became known as the *Moving Statues*. Night after night people gathered to see the *Moving Statues*. I witnessed the *Moving Statues*. I didn't believe it was miraculous, but I certainly witnessed the phenomenon. It was interesting that at that time there was a huge devotion in Ireland to the miraculous events happening in Medjugorje. Back then foreign holidays or sun holidays were not the norm for Irish people, yet tens of thousands of faithful Irish flew to Medjugorje, to witness the *Miracle of the Sun*.

In the context of *Begotten Not Made*, it occurred to me as interesting that people could be so accepting of miraculous interventions by Our Lady, yet the idea that St. Joseph might appear from heaven would be considered incredible, far-fetched, farcical if not outrageous.

CM: Very interesting, indeed. St Joseph appearing to the nun is outlandish.

CC: I mean it was outrageous in the context of the characters in the book who had devoted their lives to so many other extreme beliefs including, resurrection from the dead, walking on water, virgin births, miraculous cures, apparitions of saints, devils transforming into snakes. Yet, the young Brother Scully's faith will only stretch so far, and the notion of St. Joseph appearing to a dying nun was just a belief too far. – *"Really, whoever heard of St. Joseph ever appearing to anyone?!"* (CREEDON 2018, 105).

CM: Ok. I've been rereading the passages linking Brother Scully with Ambrose. And this is where the Herod theory resumes. I found the theological debate here much more vibrant and liberating. I felt the two were discussing on the same level, on a friendly level, despite their different opinions. It was therefore really frustrating to realise that Ambrose had already decided to take his life.

CC: Yes, I do think Brother Ambrose and Brother Scully totally enjoyed the heated discussion, despite the seriousness of it. It was a debate that had been on the cards since Brother Scully was in the seminary, but it took some years before he would be informed and skilled enough to challenge the Master of Theology, Brother Ambrose. In boxing parlance, it was a Title Fight and Scully took the Title in the thirteenth round.

CM: I don't understand why the Brothers were considered inferior to priests, as it is hinted at by Brother Ambrose.

CC: It's more than hinted. It's understood that Brothers and nuns are at the bottom of the pyramid of power. The Christian Brothers were fundamentally established to educate underprivileged children. They were a strict religious order but had none of the perks we associate with priesthood. Christian Brothers were more or less secular, they didn't have the authority to say mass or hear confession or administer other Catholic rites. They lived under a strict vow of communal poverty and celibacy. Whereas, many priests lived comparatively privileged lives. Christian Brothers were recruited from Christian Brother schools, so for the most part Christian Brothers traditionally came from poorer, working-class backgrounds.

Christian Brothers may not have had the same liberty or religious power as priests, but yet the Christian Brothers as an organisation did have greater social and political power than any individual priest, probably due to the fact that many former students of the Christian Brothers went on to hold high-powered positions in the civil service, semi-state sectors and politics, and of course right across the country the Christian Brothers had a network and were a substantial voting bloc – and politicians would be very aware of this.

I went to the North Monastery Christian Brothers, and I guess in my mind's eye the topography of *Begotten Not Made* suggests that Brother Scully was in the North Monastery and Sister Claire was in the adjacent North Presentation Convent. You know the North Monastery, Conci. I remember you did a course there one summer maybe back in 2001?

CM: Yes, I know it very well.
The North Monastery also features in your documentary films?

CC: As I mentioned earlier in this interview, my Gods have always been local, and my heroes ate chester cake and supped milk at our shop counter.

My film documentaries cover the same ground, but the emphasis is on presenting real stories of real people accurately. My documentary making informs my fiction, just as much as my fiction informs my documentary making. My documentary projects usually come out of endless research of a person, an institution, an organization, or an event in history which has specific resonance with my neighbourhood. It gets to the point when my research becomes overwhelming and at that point, I feel the need to record it. The need to record becomes almost obsessive. I encounter some fascinating individuals in the course of my research, and I realise if I don't record these individuals they will be lost to history, lost to local memory. Michael Crane the pigeon fancier [*The Boys of Fair Hill*[13]] is one of those individuals. Claire Ormond O'Driscoll [*If It's Spiced Beef, It Must Be Christmas*[14]] is another; John O'Shea [*The Boys of Fairhill*]; Anna Grace [*Flynnie, the Man Who Walked Like Shakespeare*[15]]; Arthur Dowling [*Why The Guns Remained Silent in Rebel Cork*[16]]; Máire MacSwiney Brugha [*The Burning of Cork*[17]]. It is often the case that the people telling a story are more important than the story they tell. I guess that goes back to our shop counter when growing up. I more or less move in with these people, calling to their house, just sitting at their table talking endlessly. For me the documentary becomes secondary and is ultimately a by-product of the encounters I have with these amazing people I meet along the way.

The subjects of the documentary are obviously a primary focus. The now legendary figure of Father O' Flynn and his work in the Shandon area may have slipped by unnoticed unless his story was recorded while his peers were still alive. Similarly, *The Burning Of Cork* is now recognised as an event of national importance, and this year [pre-Covid-19] there were many plans for centenary celebrations, including screenings in New York, Belfast, Dublin, Cork among other places. But back in 2005, when I was researching this story, the event was relatively unknown even here in Cork. Hard to believe there wasn't even as much as an echo of that catastrophic event. It certainly was not given any real space in the history books. I remember coming across a one-line mention of the Burning of Cork in a school history

---

13 *The Boys of Fairhill*, RTÉ 2007. https://www.youtube.com/watch?v=LxChF__cCtI.
14 *If It's Spiced Beef, It Must Be Christmas*, RTÉ 2007. https://www.youtube.com/watch?v=VTborcen3eA&t=1406s.
15 *Flynnie, The Man Who Walked Like Shakespeare*, RTÉ, 2008. https://www.youtube.com/watch?v=2CuauTBACUo&t=.
16 *Why The Guns Remained Silent In Rebel Cork*, RTÉ 2006. https://www.youtube.com/watch?v=X59c4egVjJI&t=715s.
17 *The Burning of Cork*, RTÉ, 2005. https://www.youtube.com/watch?v=4TFGn_KiVUU&t=702s.

book, but even in that the substantial details were incorrect, including the year it happened. There was little or no collective memory, information, or record of this event, even City Hall had no mention of it on the City Council website.

It is so satisfying now, fifteen years later, to encounter the many books and television programmes on the subject, and the way the city has embraced it as a cornerstone moment on our history timeline. I do derive a certain amount of personal pride from that. Similarly, I do feel a certain amount of personal achievement that my theory of Major Geoff Compton-Smith as the inspiration for Frank O'Connor's story *Guests of the Nation,* is now accepted – recently referenced in the Irish Times (An Irishman's Diary), obviously I wasn't credited – but that doesn't matter, it was nice to see that my research is accepted and now part of the greater national narrative.

This might sound like a stupid thing to say, but I only want to make documentaries about stories I want to tell. I am regularly invited to make documentaries, but invariably I turn them down. I guess I really have no interest in making television programmes for the sake of making television programmes. I am only interested in telling my own stories.

If I can tell a story I want to tell, and if that elevates some aspect of my neighbourhood to local, national or international significance, well that's all the better.

CM: You are basically a researcher inside the texture of life in Cork.

CC: Researcher might be too strong a word. I'm certainly not an academic. I am fascinated by people and the stories they tell. But then there's a huge part of me that just loves writing pure fiction for fiction's sake. I love that sense of trawling through my own brain and imagining bizarre situations and characters. But I do like to record aspects of life and acknowledge the cultural significance of what is often side-lined and considered to be marginal by more mainstream culture.

Cónal Creedon outside No1 Launderette Devonshire Street, Cork 1989
© Barry Fitzgerald.

I really have no interest in nostalgia; my aim is to bring these hidden but living traditions to the attention of the general public.

CM: You have reached your quest, both within the text and as a general idea!

CC: Ah, well I wouldn't say it was a quest, it's just me trying to put some logical answer or explanation to your questions regarding why I do what I seem to instinctively do ...

Conci, you have probably seen *If It's Spiced Beef, It Must Be Christmas*, my documentary about the traders who live and work in my part of town. The people featured in it are friends and neighbours of mine. I guess we began by talking about inspiration. I'm not sure if inspiration is the right word, but those shops and shopkeepers are ingrained in my life. I don't view them as some quaint oddity, they are fundamental, the lifeblood and beating heart of my existence.

For example, Tony Linehan's Sweet Factory is referenced in the final passage of *Passion Play* as part of Pluto's vision of heaven. It's mentioned a few times in my play *The Cure*. A scene in my play *When I Was God* is set in Linehan's Sweet Factory where the character is talking to Danny Linehan, Tony's dad. Linehan's also features in my documentary about Father O' Flynn, *Flynnie, The Man Who Walked Like Shakespeare*, and it is a major part of my documentary, *If It's Spiced Beef, It Must Be Christmas* – it crops up again and again in various places of my writing. You talk about maps and locations in my work, well it is actually these incidental references that hold up a true mirror to my life, my insights, my inspiration – rather than any Ordinance Survey quality street map.

I'm not sure if inspiration is the correct word, but I often think Paddy Kavanagh's poem *Epic* – totally captures where my head is. Though I am aware of globally significant individuals and events and history and culture, I am most engaged by the unfolding events and characters who inhabit my own personal, almost private, local globe. Paddy Kavanagh refers to the lead-up to World War II as "the Munich bother" and dismisses it in the context of the importance of a local land dispute between two subsistence farmers McCabe and Duffy. And I guess that's where I am. My world is my street. I believe that even if I could live for two lifetimes, I still won't have time to discover or understand every facet of my world.

Epic, Patrick Kavanagh (1960)

I have lived in important places, times
When great events were decided; who owned
That half a rood of rock, a no-man's land
Surrounded by our pitchfork-armed claims.
I heard the Duffy's shouting "Damn your soul!"
And old McCabe stripped to the waist, seen
Step the plot defying blue cast-steel –
"Here is the march along these iron stones"
That was the year of the Munich bother.
Which was more important? I inclined
To lose my faith in Ballyrush and Gortin
Till Homer's ghost came whispering to my mind.
He said: I made the Iliad from such
A local row. Gods make their own importance.

CM: *Talking about the fairy tales Dowcha Boy and the story of Mossie and Sister Francesca, why did you use so much irony? I particularly liked when he "decided to walk with his wings folded behind his back chirping a tune like a local French pigeon from Picardie"* (CREEDON 2018, 94).

CC: The Dowcha Boy story appears relatively early in the text, it seemed like the type of story that would interest a young seminarian from the Northside of Cork City. It was also a major leap away from the world of convent and monastic life and I thought it would be good to bring the readers out over the walls for a little jaunt. But most of all, it's in there because I really enjoyed writing it, it made me laugh. And believe it or not, I often laugh as I'm writing, it's as if I've heard something funny for the first time. And conversely, I've been known to shed a tear. In, *Begotten Not Made* I find the scene where Mossie the Gardener insists on time alone with the dying love of his life to be very moving. I also find the moment when Brother Scully eventually meets Sister Claire after fifty years gets me every time. And in *Passion Play* there is always a misty-eyed moment when Pluto walks away from Tragic Ted in Piccadilly – something about walking away from a self-destructive friend I find so profoundly sad.

But back to the pigeon... I guess, I wanted to put that sense of cleverness in the pigeon or in the storytelling about the pigeon, so the pigeon deceived the German guards by pretending to be a local French pigeon by whistling a song about a local area in France. It's just stressing that sense of place, that sense of home that seems so important to humans, but in this case imposing it on a pigeon – ironically, a homing pigeon.

CM: Is there a similar structure in Passion Play *and* Begotten Not Made?

CC: In one way the two books are totally different. *Passion Play* is chaotically episodic, while *Begotten Not Made* is extremely linear. But now that I'm forced to think about it, I realize the two books are incredibly similar. To begin with the two books take place over one full day. And the day is the eve of a very important celebration in the Christian calendar; Good Friday and Christmas – the death and birth of Jesus Christ respectively.

The two main protagonists spend that full day confined to a room, the room in both books is cell-like, both characters are afraid to leave their respective rooms, both characters have serious emotional and psychiatric problems, both protagonists are living with a sense of love lost. Jesus! Maybe they are totally autobiographical! [*Laughing out loud here*]

So, they create a whole life, a world within the room. But eventually both Brother Scully and Pluto realize they must leave the room in order to find some sort of redemption, internal calm and resolution and put the world right. I'm laughing here, when I say, I must read those books again and find out more about myself.

CM: In the video interview where did you read the pages from Passion Play? *So, the places Pluto is describing as his view of heaven are actually in the background. I walked up there last Easter. It was stunning! I did it very slowly taking pictures while I was going up. Yes, from there you have an immense wonder magic view.*

CC: Regarding the extract from *Passion Play* in the film clip, I am reading in the location where the text is set – the final scene in *Passion Play* unfolds in Bell's Field on the top of Patrick's Hill.

And absolutely, this is Pluto's vision of heaven. The point being that this place, this 'city of pain' that drove Pluto to take his own life is also his heaven. Heaven and hell are two sides of the same coin. It's a matter of perspective.

By the way, this location, Bell's Field is also the location of the crucifixion scene in my millennium pageant *The Trial of Jesus.*[18]

CM: Narrative versus Character – discuss your thoughts?

CC: To tell you the truth, Conci, my writing is basically about me trying to figure out my observations of a lifetime. Writing for me is all about the process. Realistically, publication is not that important to me, except there comes a time when I have developed a world and characters on paper, and obviously I then publish the book or have the play produced. Even my film documentaries are really a self-exploration.

My fiction is totally driven by characterization. Similarly, my documentaries are all about developing characters, and if a character is strong enough the narrative only gets in the way. A well-defined character will expose/explore a narrative even if he/she is only going to buy a bottle of milk. I feel if the narrative is too strong, in other

18   See https://www.youtube.com/watch?v=aS3hlFvicLk.

Plate from Begotten Not Made. Silhouette drawing by Cónal Creedon.

words if it's all about the story, well then the writing can become like painting by numbers, joining the dots and filling in the narrative blanks.

CM: The Cure (2005) is my favourite play, I felt I could follow the grandfather's nose up through Cork. Once I thought that it could be interpreted by a dancer while somebody was reading this part of the play!

CC: Interesting you should say that. It was first performed by Mikel Murfi – an actor who brings a lot of mime and movement to his performance.

My personal favourite play of the *Second City Trilogy* is *After Luke*, and audiences seem to prefer *When I was God*. Then again, *The Cure* is the most personal of the three. The character actually walks past my house in the play, twice – you don't get more personal than that. But there's something about *After Luke* that I just love – the three-way dynamic of actors on stage.

CM: China has been an important haven of your literary career – can you tell us about your experience there?
CC: Over the years I have presented many lectures, stage plays and screenings of my documentaries in China. It's a relationship that came about in an organic way. I was in China in 2009 for a three-month residency with the Shanghai Writers' Association. I had been there the previous year as a guest of the Shanghai International Literary Festival. While I was on the residency there, people had seen the reviews of my New York productions in the New York Times. The word went out among the international community that I was in Shanghai, and before I knew it, I was collaborating with the Shanghai Repertory Theatre Company. I went back the following year with two of my plays *When I Was God* and *After Luke* which were performed at the Shanghai World Expo. Then I returned in 2011 for the Shanghai JUE Festival with another one of my plays, *The Cure*. And I performed a series of concerts there with John Spillane in 2013. The Chinese Writers' Association invited me back as guest of honour in 2018.

Coming from Cork, China was such an immense culture shock. It absolutely woke me up. I've come to know many Chinese writers and performers at this point, and it has always been a positive and enhancing experience. I am very grateful for the twists of fate that brought me to China's shore. China has taught me so much about myself, it has offered me an incredible perspective on my working life in Cork. It's very liberating to know that there is a whole world out there, and the realization that a few city blocks in Shanghai represent a population larger than the total population of Cork, really puts life in perspective.

Long before I ever had any idea, plan or interest in going to China, a decade earlier, back in 1999, the international community in Beijing produced a special publication to celebrate the millennium. They requested a story from me which I submitted to them. Some months later, when the publication arrived in the post from China, I was delighted and well honoured to realize that they had only included two writers. I was one – the other was Seamus Heaney. That was a special moment.

CM: Was there any significant event while you've been touring around to read from Begotten Not Made?

CC: Ah sur' listen, every reading is a potential pantomime, there is an aspect of every single live performance that is a learning curve. I've been at readings where scuffles have broken out. I love giving readings, I do suffer from extreme nerves right up to the moment I open my mouth and then it's like an alter ego kicks in – I just roll with it and it's liable to end up anywhere.

But speaking of Seamus Heaney. A few years back, I was reading at Bantry Library, and lo and behold, who turned up at the reading only, Seamus Heaney. Totally unexpected. Seamus is from the far north of Ireland and Bantry is on the furthermost south coast of Ireland. It just so happened he was in Bantry that day, so he dropped in to the reading.

I decided to cut my reading short and invite him up to read. Of course, everyone wanted him to read, but he didn't have any of his own books with him. I think he was just being a gentleman and not wishing to cast a shadow on my limelight. But I pointed out that we were in a library, and they had all his books on the shelf, so up he came and read from his work. Really it was such a brilliant and fun afternoon. It's the magic of live performance that readings often take on an unexpected turn, keeps it a little bit rock 'n' roll. It was fun, off the cuff, and unexpected, and I like that. We all retired to Ma

Murphy's pub after that – songs were sung, and mighty fun was had.

CM: *A very happy coincidence together in the Chinese Millennium celebration and together at the reading in Bantry, pure coincidence and such sweet memories.*

CC: Isn't that what life's all about? Making sweet memories is the way forward!

CM: *Have you employed different language registers, Cork Hibernian English, according to the various characters both in* Passion Play *and in* Begotten Not Made?

CC: Not sure of your question, but if you are wondering if I use different styles of language, micro-dialects, I do. Maybe it's because I have written so much radio, but I'm subconsciously extremely conscious of having different voice modulations. I can look at a page of dialogue and tell who's speaking, not by the words but by the very length of the sentences. We all speak in very individualistic ways, and if I can tune into that enough it means I can dispense with much of the: *he said, she said,* and worst of all, *he said wistfully.* Let the language flow.

I find that there is a whole genre of fiction that portrays working-class characters in a dark world of drug taking, prostitution, crime, speaking with coarse language, so I decided to do a total flip on that and explore a working class that is universally more educated.

Christian Brothers are recruited from working-class families. So basically, I was presenting a character with a working-class morality, culture, background, values, but with the added bonus of being educated. So, it was presenting working-class values, but with a more educated understanding.

CM: *As Walter Benjamin said: "Work on good prose has three steps: a musical stage when it is composed, an architectonic one when it is built, and a textile one when it is woven". I find that your novel has got a rhythmic scaffolding, at times its text runs very fast, especially in*

roller-coaster dialogues, then it takes a breath, especially in contempla-
tive views from Brother Scully's window, what can you tell me about the
musicality of your novel?

CC: No less than any other writer, I do like to include an aural rhythm, metre and even sometimes I'll dip into a slight rhyme, or the bounce I can achieve by slipping in an echo of repetition and alliteration. The truth of the matter is that it's very easy to overindulge the flowery nature of words on a page, that can kill dead the spontaneity of the prose. So, I also work at not making it appear too contrived on the page. The ideal is that it should read lyrically when read out loud. I guess some would call aspiring to achieve that balance is the *work* of being a writer – I'm inclined to call it the *joy* of being a writer.

CM: Cónal, I feel I must thank you for giving me this precious oppor-
tunity to interview you online, we probably invented a new method! It
has added value to my lockdown. I feel I have been able to go 'Beyond
visible, beyond your visible world'.

CC: Thank you, Conci, for taking the time to unravel my contorted thoughts and putting them into a logical order. I look forward to seeing you next time you are in Cork. We'll go for a walk. I'm looking forward to seeing more of your photography – it seems to me, partic-ularly during Covid, the power of the visual image has come into its own. Best regards to you, Conci – I look forward to seeing you in Cork someday when these dreadful days are a thing of the past.

Works Cited

CREEDON Cónal (1995), *Pancho And Lefty Ride Out*, Cork, Collins Press.

— (1999), *Passion Play*, Dublin, Poolbeg Press [2nd ed., Cork, Irishtown Press 2017].

— (2007), *The Second City Trilogy*, Cork, Irishtown Press.

— (2015), *The Immortal Deed of Michael O'Leary*, Cork, Cork City Libraries-Leabharlanna Cathrach Chorcaí.

— ed., (2016), *Cornerstone*, Cork, Cork City Libraries-Leabharlanna Cathrach Chorcaí /University College Cork.

— (2018) *Begotten Not Made*, Cork, Irishtown Press.

Photo: Clare Keogh

Biography

Presented with: *The Leonardo da Vinci World Award of Arts 2024*
[The World Cultural Council, Switzerland].
The Irish Books, Arts & Music Award 2024
[American Irish Heritage Centre, Chicago].

Cónal Creedon is a novelist, playwright and documentary film maker.

His collection of short fiction, Pancho And Lefty Ride Again (2021) was awarded One City One Book 2022, and The Bronze Award Next Generation Book Awards USA 2022 (Finalist). His novel, *Begotten Not Made* (2018), has achieved literary award recognition: the Eric Hoffer Award USA 2020, the Bronze Award Next Generation Book Awards USA 2020, Finalist in the Montaigne [Most Thought-Provoking Book] Award USA 2020, Nominated for the Dublin International Book Award 2020. Book of the Year Irish Examiner 2020. Top Books of the Year – Liveline RTÉ Irish National Radio. Other books by Cónal Creedon include, *Cornerstone* (2017), *The Immortal Deed of Michael O'Leary* (2015), *Second City Trilogy* (2007), *Passion Play* (1999) cited as Book of the Year BBC Radio 4, *Pancho And Lefty Ride Out* (1995).

Award-winning plays include; *The Trial of Jesus* (2000), which featured as part of the Irish National Millennium celebrations, received two Business to Arts Awards by President of Ireland, Mary McAleese and was nominated for an Irish Times Special Judges Theatre Award 2000. *Glory Be To The Father* (2001), produced by Red Kettle Theatre Company, Waterford. Cónal's *Second City Trilogy* of stage plays achieved high acclaim from theatre critics in Shanghai, New York and Ireland. *The Second City Trilogy* picked up several awards at the 1st Irish Theatre Awards New York, including Best Actor, Best Director and nominated Best Playwright. *When I Was God*, from the *Second City Trilogy* was also awarded Best Actor and Best Supporting Actor at ICA Federation Awards 2014. In 2021 it was awarded Best Production, Best Actor and Best Director at the Irish National Play Awards.

Cónal's film documentaries achieved high critical acclaim – shortlisted for the Focal International Documentary Awards UK and numerous broadcasts by RTÉ [Irish National Television] with international screenings at Féile an Phobail West Belfast Festival, World Expo Shanghai, China, Origin Theatre Festival New York, USA, the Irish National Centenary Commemorations and at NYU New York University, USA.

Cónal has written and produced more than 60 hours of original radio drama broadcast by RTÉ, BBC, CBC, ABC. Cited as Best Radio by Irish Times radio critics 1996 and 1998.

Recognition for Contribution to the Arts

- Presented with The Leonardo da Vinci World Award of Arts 2024 [The World Cultural Council, Switzerland].
- Presented with The Irish Books, Arts & Music Award 2024 [American Irish Heritage Centre, Chicago].
- Cumann Iarscoláirí na Mainistreach Thuaidh. Person of The Year Award 2021
- Appointed (Covid-Pandemic) Goodwill Literary Ambassador for Cork City 2020
- Awarded Lord Mayor's Culture Award 2020
- Appointed Culture Ambassador for Cork City 2020
- Invited Guest of Honour, 10th Anniversary Shanghai Writers' China 2018
- Nominated Cork Person of the Year 2018
- Appointed Adjunct Professor of Creative Writing UCC 2017
- Appointed Heritage Ambassador for Cork City 2017
- Keynote Speaker Daniel Corkery Summer School, Inchigeela, Ireland 2016
- Keynote Speaker Merriman Summer School, Glór, Ennis, Ireland 2015
- Keynote Speaker Launch Cork Europa Erlesen, Irish Embassy Berlin, Germany 2014
- Invited Scholarship Forum, Fudan University, Shanghai, China 2008
- Invited Speaker 7-City Reading Tour, Irish American Cultural Institute, USA 2008
- Nominated Cork Person of the Year 2001
- Awarded Lord Mayor's Culture Award 1999

Theatre

2021   *When I Was God – Special Covid Production – The Irish National Play Awards. Awarded Best Production, Best Actor and Best Director at Irish National Play Awards*

2019   *The Cure – Arlene's Grocery, New York*

2016   *The Cure – Irish Arts Centre Queens, New York*

2014   *When I Was God – Fletcher and Camross Drama. ICI Festival Awarded Best Actor. ICI Federation Drama Festival Awards Awarded Best Supporting Actor. ICI Federation Drama Awards*

2013   *The Cure – USA Premiere. Green Room Theatre New York Awarded Best Actor. 1st Irish Theatre Awards New York Nominated Best Playwright. 1st Irish Theatre Awards New York*

2011   *The Cure – JUE International Arts Festival, Shanghai. China*

2011   *The Cure – Halfmoon Theatre. Cork Opera House. Ireland*

2010   *When I Was God & After Luke Chinese Premiere, Shanghai World Expo*

2010   *When I Was God & After Luke – Cork Arts Theatre. Ireland*

2009   *When I Was God & After Luke – (Irish Rep Theatre New York) Awarded Best Director 1st Irish Theatre Awards New York Nominated Best Actor 1st Irish Theatre Awards New York Nominated Best Production 1st Irish Theatre Awards New York*

2008   *When I Was God – USA Premiere [Green Room New York)*

2005   *The Cure – Cork Opera House/ Blood in the Alley Theatre Co.*

2005   *After Luke – Cork Opera House/Blood in the Alley Theatre Co.*

2005   *The Second City Trilogy – Comm European Capital of Culture*

2002   *When I Was God – Madder Market, 3 Cities Festival, Norwich, UK*

2001   *Glory Be To The Father – Red Kettle Theatre Company National Tour: Waterford, Kilkenny, Cork, Galway, Sligo*

2001   *When I Was God – Everyman Palace Theatre, Cork, Ireland*

2001   *When I Was God – Bewley's Theatre, Dublin, Ireland*

2000   *The Trial Of Jesus – Corcadorca Theatre Company. Featured as part of the National Millennium Celebrations. Awarded two National Business to Arts Awards. Nominated for Irish Times Theatre Awards*

1999   *When I Was God – Red Kettle Theatre Company*

Books

2021   *Pancho And Lefty Ride Again – a collection of short fiction published*
by Irishtown Press Ltd.
– Awarded One City One Book 2022
– Finalist Next Generation Book Awards USA 2022

2018   *Begotten Not Made – a novel published by Irishtown Press Ltd.*
– Awarded the Eric Hoffer Award for commercial fiction 2020, USA
– Bronze Award in NGBA Book Awards 2019, USA
– Finalist the Montaigne Award 'Most Thought-Provoking Book'
2020, USA
– Listed for the Dublin International Book Award 2020 (to be
announced)
– Shortlisted for Readers Favourite Book Awards 2018, USA.
– Cited as Best Book of the Year – Irish Examiner.
– Listed as Books to Read for 2020 – Liveline RTÉ.

2017   *Cornerstone – Editor of anthology of UCC student writing.*
Published by UCC & Cork City Libraries.

2015   *Immortal Deed Of Michael O'Leary – pub. by Cork City Libraries.*

2007   *Second City Trilogy – a trilogy of internationally award-winning*
stage plays, published by Irishtown Press ltd. Commissioned by
European Capital of Culture 2005. Productions in China, USA
and Ireland.
Awarded Best Director. 1st Irish Theatre Awards New York, 2009.
Nominated Best Production. 1st Irish Theatre Awards New York,
2009.
Awarded Best Actor. 1st Irish Theatre Awards New York, 2013.
Nominated Best Playwright. 1st Irish Theatre Awards New York,
2013.
Awarded Best Actor. ICI Federation Drama Festival Awards, 2014.
Awarded Best Supporting Actor. ICI Federation Drama Festival
Awards, 2014.

1999	*Passion Play – a novel cited as,*
	– Book of the Year (BBC Radio 4)
	– Book of the Week (The Irish Examiner)
	– Book on One (RTÉ 1 – Irish National Radio)
	– Book of the Week (RAI – Italian National Radio)
	Translated into Italian, Bulgarian with extracts published in Germany, China.
1995	*Pancho And Lefty Ride Out – a collection of short stories. pub. The Collins Press. Short stories have been adapted for stage, film and radio.*
	Short stories have been published and broadcast extensively in news-papers, magazines, literary periodicals and collections.
	With translation into German, and China – Cónal's short fiction gained recognition in
	– Life Extra Short Story Awards,
	– Francis Mac Manus Short Story Awards,
	– George A. Birmingham Short Story Awards,
	– One-Voice Monologue Awards BBC
	– The PJ O'Connor Awards.

Radio Drama

Cónal has penned over 60 hours of original fiction, short stories and plays, for radio. His work has represented Ireland in the World Play International Radio Drama Festival 2000 and was subsequently broadcast on participating networks: BBC Radio 4, ABC (Australia), RTHK (Hong Kong), LATW (USA), CBC (Canada), BBC World Service, RNZ (New Zealand), RTÉ.

2005	*Adventure of the Downtown Dirty Faces. (5 short stories – RTÉ Radio)*
2005	*No. 1, Devonshire Street (BBC Radio 4 & BBC World Service)*
2004	*Adaptation – Tailor and Ansty (RTÉ Drama)*
2004	*Passion Play – Book on One. (RTÉ Radio)*
2003	*The Prodigal Maneen (Awarded the C of I Bursary RTÉ)*
2003	*Adaptation – Guests of the Nation (Frank O' Connor Centenary – RTÉ)*
2002	*The Cure (Monologue – RTÉ)*
2001	*1601 The March of O'Sullivan Beara (Docu/drama Battle of Kinsale)*
2000	*This Old Man, He Played One (World Play International Fest.)*
1994-98	*Under the Goldie Fish (85 half-hour episodes – RTÉ)*
	Listed one of Best Radio Programmes in 1996 & 1998 – The Irish Times.
1994	*After the Ball (Francis MacManus Awards)*
1994	*Every Picture Tells a Story (RTÉ Radio 1)*
1994	*Caught in a Trap (C.L.R Drama Competition RTÉ)*
1993	*Come Out Now, Hacker Hanley! (RTÉ Radio)*

TV Documentary/ Film

2010   *Flynnie, The Man Who Walked Like Shakespeare (Producer/writer/*
        director).
        Nominated Focal Documentary Awards. London, UK.
2007   *The Boys Of Fairhill (Producer/writer/director) Screened RTÉ.*
2006   *If It's Spiced Beef (Producer/writer/director) Screened RTÉ.*
2006   *Why The Guns Remained Silent In Rebel Cork (Writer/director)*
        Screened RTÉ.
2005   *The Burning of Cork (Writer/director)*
        Screened RTE. Cork Archives. Cork City Hall & World Expo Shanghai
        2010.
        NYU (New York University) USA, West Belfast Festival, Origin Theatre
        New York USA.
        Public screening as part of the official Irish Government Centenary
        Celebrations.
2001   *A Man of Few Words (Short film produced by Indie Films)*
        Screened on RTÉ & various film festivals.
1995   *The Changing Faces of Ireland. RTÉ (co-scripted six-part series)*
        Screened on RTÉ.

Recorded Collaborations

Collaborations include:
- Singer songwriter John Spillane
- Singer-songwriter Claire Sands
- Small Birds [Sound Artists: Irene Murphy, Mick O'Shea & Harry Moore] – One City One Book. 2022
- Orchestral composer, John O'Brien, and Cork Opera House Orchestra. 2021
- DJs Greg D and Shane Johnson– Fish Go Deep, Magic Night by The Lee. 2021

Other

- Writer-in-Residence University College Cork. 2016
- Writer-in-Residence Shanghai Writers' Association 2008
- Writer-in-Residence Cork Everyman Palace. 1999–2001
- Radio presenter for RTÉ & columnist with The Irish Times. 1999–2001
- Writer-in-Residence Cork County Council. 1998
- Writer-in-Residence Cork Prison 1997

Special – Covid Online-Streaming Presentation/Productions

March 2022	*Knowledge: International institute of Influencers conference, IMS Law College Noida, India*
Feb 2022	*Creativity: Humanities, University of Rajasthan, Jaipur, India*
Dec 2021	*Present Artistic practice lecture IMS Law College Noida, India*
July 2021	*The Writer's Mindset – with Yvonne Reddin. Dublin Ireland*
June 2021 a.	*Cork City Hall, conference: Senior Chinese officials Program 2021, China*
June 2021 b.	*Cork City Hall, conference: Senior Chinese officials Program 2021, China*
May 2021	*LITREAL: The New Standard. Interviewed by Dr Shasikala Palsamy, India*
April 2021	*World Book Day, with Tina Pisco and Sara Baume. World Book Day*
March 2021	*St. Patrick's Day – The Traditions of St Patrick. The Crawford Gallery*
March 2021	*The Cure – Online streaming [Covid-19] Everyman Palace Theatre*
March 2021	*When I Was God – Online streaming – Everyman Palace Theatre*
March 2021	*After Luke – Online streaming – Everyman Palace Theatre*
Feb 2021	*Screening – Burning of Cork – 1st Irish Theatre Festival New York*
Feb 2021	*Yan Ge, Museum of Literature Ireland, Dublin. Chinese New Year*
Dec 2020	*Public Reading commemoration of Burning of Cork – Cork City Hall*
Dec 2020	*Screening of documentary – Burning of Cork – Cork City Hall*
Dec 2020	*Concert with John Spillane – Everyman Palace Theatre*
Nov 2020	*The Cure – Online streaming, Everyman Palace Theatre*
Nov 2020	*When I Was God – Online streaming, Everyman Palace Theatre*
Nov 2020	*After Luke – Online streaming, Everyman Palace Theatre*
Sept 2020	*Online film – Flavours of Cork – European Association – SPD – EU*
July 2020	*Filmed discussion: Story of portrait by Eileen Healy – Crawford Gallery Cork*
July 2020	*Féile an Phobail, documentary streamed and interview – Belfast*
June 2020	*Green Room – concert Cónal Creedon and John Spillane – Cork Opera House*

Reading Tours include

Switzerland	James Joyce Foundation Zurich 2020.
	Centre for Irish Studies Zurich University 2020
Italy	4 city Reading tour Italy – 2001.
	Rome, Florence, Venice, Perugia.
UK	Various reading tours.
	Dylan Thomas Centre – Swansea. 2000.
	Filthy McNasty's – London. 2001.
	Madder Market Theatre – 3 Cities Festival – Norwich. 2002.
China	Presented several reading tours to Shanghai, China.
	Shanghai International Literary Festival. 2008.
	Fudan Uni. Shanghai, People's Uni. Shanghai, Le Chéile Shanghai. 2009.
	Shanghai World Expo. 2010.
	Shanghai Jue International Arts Festival. 2010.
	M on the Bund & Shanghai Writer's Association. 2013.
	Guest of Honour – 10th Anniversary – Shanghai Writers' Association 2017.
USA	Irish American Cultural Institute, 7 city coast-to-coast reading tour USA. 2007.
	New York, Albany, Rochester, Omaha, Montana, San Francisco, New Jersey.
	NYU – New York University 2019.
Austria	Sprachsalz Literary Festival. Tyrol Austria. 2014.
Berlin	Launch of Cork Europa Erlesen – Translated by Jürgen Schneider. 2016.
	The Literaturwerkstatt Berlin festival 2011
Ireland	Numerous readings at literary festivals – Including,
	Keynote Speaker at Daniel Corkery Summer School. 2019.
	Speaker at Merriman Summer School. 2014.

Selection of Reviews

Good writing knows no ethnicity. Good writing knows no nationality. Good writing is good writing – not alone is this good writing - It's excellent writing. Very personal writing. Very humorous writing. They say if Dublin was burnt down it could be rebuilt again by reading the work of James Joyce – well the very same could be said about Creedon's work – Cork city could be built from his words.

Malachy McCourt – WBAI RADIO New York

The novel's interior is much indebted to Joyce. The way Creedon combines the child-centred perspective of *Paddy Clarke Ha! Ha! Ha!* with the tough teenage world of *The Commitments* and the domestic cruelty of *The Woman Who Walked into Doors* is ambitious and effective. His exposition of his characters' thought processes owes much to Flann O' Brien's skewed sophistication and Patrick McCabe's scabrous vision as to an earlier prototype of Seán O' Casey's Joxer. Creedon has found a form all of his own.

C.L. Dallat, Times Literary Review [TLS]

Fathers and sons and the damage done: this is the theme, with variations, of the Cork writer Cónal Creedon's fine plays *After Luke* and *When I Was God*, which can be seen in a nearly pitch-perfect production. Mr Creedon's words are enough to create a world that is at once comic and dramatic, poetic and musical.

Rachel Saltz, New York Times.

The highlight of last year's theatre in Shanghai came all the way from Cork in Irish playwright's Cónal Creedon's double-header of short plays – powerful, yet punctuated with humour, lyrical and richly colloquial. They were terrific!

That's Shanghai Magazine [China].

Irish playwrights (from Yeats and Wilde and Synge and Shaw on down to now) are always good going on great, and the latest in that endless chain is all but unknown in America, Cónal Creedon. Unknown no longer, Creedon's short, idiosyncratic *After Luke*, and even shorter, punchier *When I Was God*, comprise a disturbing two-hour double-bill. Idiosyncratic? Bite off any hunk of either work; it's all as chewy as leather yet weirdly digestible. None of this would be unfamiliar to, let's say, D. H. Lawrence, or, for that matter, George Orwell. What hasn't been heard before is the thorny voice of 48-year-old Cónal Creedon of County Cork, Ireland, who, from all reports, is a lot gentler in the flesh than on paper.

Jerry Tallmer, New York Villager.

They were discussing what should go into the Irish Millennium Time-Capsule. If they are looking for something to represent Ireland, how about Cónal Creedon's *Under the Goldie Fish*? It's so off the wall, that it shouldn't ring true, but the most frightening fact is that it does...

Eilís O'Hanlon, The Sunday Independent.

This is contemporary theatre that plays like the works of a past master. The work of Irish playwright Cónal Creedon, are quite simply a delight, [but] not in an all-sunshine and light way. On a sparse stage on which the characters can only live or die, it lives. Underlying all is a love of language and a keen observance of detail – Creedon is lyrical, and uses rhyme and rhythm, without being showy, and enriches with the Cork colloquial without alienating – Come back soon, you are always welcome on the Shanghai stage.

Talk Shanghai. China. Arts Editor.

As written by Cónal Creedon, such moments resound with wince-inducing authenticity before they are eclipsed by an inspirational twist – words, inflected with the faintly Scandinavian accent of Munster, soar like a bracing breeze off the River Lee.

Andy Webster, New York Times.

Under the Goldie Fish would make Gabriel García Márquez turn puce in a pique of jealousy... Gold card radio with plums on.

Tom Widger, The Sunday Tribune.

I don't know why Cónal Creedon hasn't been produced on Broadway yet. Certainly, his plays are as deserving as any recent work from Ireland that has made that cut. In fact, he has more to say, more concisely, than just about any of his dramatic contemporaries.

Cahir O'Doherty, Irish Central New York.

Vigorously sustained by stylish performances and an ingenious script, which marries comedy and pathos with a sure hand. They'll love it. It's impossible not to.
The Irish Times.

Everyone loves the Irish. It's just a fact. Creedon's script is a rich fusion of melancholy poetry and affable banter. Aidan O'Hare and *The Cure* are a match made in monologue heaven. Its potency lies in the profound ability of the playwright and the actor to connect directly with people. *The Cure* is a truly fine piece of theatre, one that is Irish to its core but anything but provincial in its scope. You couldn't ask for anything more than this.
Smart Shanghai Magazine.

Cónal Creedon's *Second City Trilogy* is a significant dramatic achievement. Creedon constructs predicaments for his characters that ring true universally. In three companion pieces that play logically together, the playwright puts a marginal view of society centre-stage, and, with warmth and humour, offers a view of life from the side lines. What ensues is a solid replaying of a classic and timeless family conflict. Taken altogether, the *Second City Trilogy* is an important a landmark in drama, its achievement is to find a theatrical language that can accommodate the poor and depressed Ireland that we have come from, and the new, confusing, complex reality we now find ourselves in. Creedon, director Geoff Gould, and the cast deserve credit not only for offering up an entertaining night of theatre, but for contributing to our understanding of where we have come from and where we are going. Any drama that can do both is indeed worthy of praise.
The Irish Examiner.

It's one of those books where it often feels inappropriate to either laugh or cry, at times surreal, frequently hilarious, often poignant but never, ever dull – The reader enters the twilight zone.
U Magazine.

Creedon can create characters, not just mouthing amusing philosophical meanderings, not just cold abstractions, these are creations of Creedon's great humanity. It is essential that I tell you here that you must finish this book. A wonderful inventive comedy.
The Sunday Tribune.

Creedon's rootedness in Cork qualifies him to chronicle the transformations that not just Cork City, but all of Ireland, caused by the economic boom of the 1990s – called the Celtic Tiger – and the aftermath. At times it feels Beckett-like, you might think the people are too unusual to exist, but they actually do.

New York City Arts.

I imagine there are few things harder to be than a contemporary Irish playwright. Given the theatrical history of the Emerald Isle, its lyric tradition, it must be either a very daring or very foolish individual indeed who steps up to be measured against the likes of the Irish literary pantheon. On the daring end falls Cónal Creedon, author of *After Luke* and *When I Was God*. The two plays are the latter parts of Creedon's serio-comic *Second City Trilogy*, focusing on life in present-day County Cork. Both plays are about the family dynamic, specifically the relationships between fathers and sons. In *After Luke*, two half-brothers, Maneen and Son, share a memory so terrible that it sets them at odds with each other all their lives. In the centre is Dadda, Maneen's father, who does his best to keep the peace but can only do so much. As he sagely says "…when two elephants go to war, 'tis the grass gets trampled."

In *When I Was God*, Dino lives in the shadow of his father's regrets, and under the pressure of his expectations. It's a classic plot, the father using the son to live the life he wished he could have had. To tell the rest would rob the reader of one of the funniest moments of the evening. Creedon's main device in these pieces is repetition. I found myself laughing uproariously as the words stayed the same, but the meaning was in constant shift, each repetition raising the stakes to a beautifully bittersweet conclusion – driving the action and the comedy. Creedon's show holds up very well against the pantheon of Irish theatre, taking chances with some very risky devices. It's a fun night out, and I'd be interested to see the trilogy in its entirety; if the first act is as entertaining as the last two, it would be well worth it.

Peter Schuyler, NY Theatre Review.

The Cure is a dramatic creation that straddles what we once were and what we have become. It examines closely the fracture at the heart of our contemporary experience – scavenging the thesaurus for sufficient superlatives for this fine piece of writing – yes, we liked it. We liked it a lot.

The Irish Examiner.

A one-man show at the Ke Center proves that you don't need a huge cast to produce a hit – their recent collaboration with Irishtown Productions proves that they are on top of their game. Cork playwright Cónal Creedon's gritty soliloquy *The Cure* saw Irish actor Aidan O'Hare command the stage as a man left behind by a racing economy and changing city. Creedon's use of language is dizzyingly attractive. He manipulates repetition to great effect, bringing the opening lines back several times in chilling sonata form. As for the staging, the Ke Center's stark space was the perfect backdrop for a bleak but redemptive piece of drama.

Asia City Network, Shanghai, China.

A pair of tenderly drawn plays by Cónal Creedon, set in Creedon's native Cork, probe the tough love and tough hurt – exchanged by men in Irish Families. Both plays – are intimately conceived and performed, tracing in chiaroscuro, the intersection between kinship and machismo.

New Yorker Magazine.

The Cure is the bittersweet tale of a man who has emotionally lost his way. As with the previous two plays, Creedon explores the frustrations of average lives, to the backdrop of historical happenings in the playwright's hometown. And as with the previous two, the script is lyrical and rich with colloquialism, the melancholy lifted with moments of delightful amusement. ("When the chemistry goes in a relationship, he reflects on marriage and drink, "There's nothing for it but to take more chemicals) – A fine piece of theatre …

That's Shanghai Magazine, Urbanatomy Shanghai.

A complex enthralling piece of theatre that boasts the dual achievement of entertaining and educating – a testament to Creedon's shrewd writing skill.

The Irish Independent.

I got to see *The Cure* at the Half Moon Theatre last night. It is terrific. It's great fun. It's just fantastic. Just so well done by Mikel Murfi. It's a credit to Cónal Creedon. Don't miss this play, you need to go and see it – the cultural highlight of Cork 2005.

Opinion Line 96fm.

Creedon's great gift seems to be observation, 45 tense, funny and pointed minutes, convincing and memorably skilful. *When I Was God*, is both a treat and a treasure.
The Irish Times.

This play operated on two levels; it was hilarious but poignant. Creedon's gift is his ability to distil the very essence of his environment. It is this sense of place and people and his gently anarchic view of life which makes his works so deliciously attractive.
The Irish Examiner.

Creedon's play shifts easily between the past and the present, revealing a sharp ear for dialogue, keen eye for observation and a deep affection for his characters as Creedon brings a deft pathos and humour to the tragicomedy of a peculiar father son relationship, a delight that demands to be savoured.
The Sunday Tribune.

BOOK OF YEAR – Highlights of the Year.
Cónal Creedon's recently published novel *Begotten Not Made* is a beguiling tale of tragic Christian Brother who forsook a potential love affair for the cloth having met a young nun on the night Dana won the Eurovision Song Contest.
Collette Sheridan – Highlights of the Year – Irish Examiner.

Selection of – BEST BOOKS OF THE YEAR.
It's a delight to read. Cónal Creedon's *Begotten Not Made*. One of the most peculiar books I have read this year.
Theo Dorgan, Liveline. RTÉ Radio 1.

READERS' FAVORITE BOOK AWARDS USA.
★ ★ ★ ★ ★ This is a work of quirky and conceptual literary fiction. For readers who enjoy fully realized, unusual lead characters, look no further – Cónal Creedon has created what feels like a real person, on whose shoulders we sit as the narration takes us deep into his life and work, his philosophy, and his sense of love in moments which are both moving, bizarre and very amusing at times. The harsh backdrop of Irish life clashes beautifully with concepts of heavenly and mortal love, miracles, and strange appearances, painting a world which is ethereal in its fairy tale moments yet painfully recognizable and relatable too. I particularly enjoyed the dynamic dialogue,

as its pacing really moves scenes along. Overall, *Begotten Not Made* is a highly recommended read for literary fiction fans searching for truly unusual books that keep you thinking long after the last page is turned.

KC Flynn, Readers' Favourite Book Awards.

US REVIEW OF BOOKS.

This book spins a delicious yarn that tips nearly every sacred cow of Christianity– a timely sport in this era of diminished participation in monastic life and the laity's scathing criticism of the Church's sins and shortcomings – all the while spotlighting the archetypal unrequited romance made fresh in the monastic setting. In the backdrop is the soul of devout Irish Catholic culture and the lives of the working-class men and women of Cork who lend a down-to-earth stability to the tale as well as zest and colour. As a bonus, the author includes his fanciful pen-and-ink drawings and tasty stories within the story, such as Sister Claire's retelling of a saga about Mossie the Gardener and his war hero pigeon, Dowcha-boy. This is a plot thread sure to tickle even the most obstinate funny bone, and it specifically lends a magical yet realistic aura to what could have been a far more level, self-conscious story.

Creedon's well-honed, multidimensional cast of characters, his vividly portrayed settings and interiors of 1970s and contemporary Cork, and his measured but lyrical prose nail every nuance of the story arc. The author has ripped open his Irish heart to spill this marvellous pastiche, a real-life creed that must be absorbed with one's heart open wide to the pathos and poignancy of love lost and found, life lived and unlived, and spirituality bound to blind faith or soaring on the wings of perception. Ultimately, Creedon's tour de force pays tribute to an end-of-life journey that paradoxically celebrates the winter of regret and the eye-opening gift of having nothing left to lose.

Kate Robinson, US Review of Books.

I thoroughly enjoyed reading *Begotten Not Made* by Cónal Creedon – it maintains a Joycean flavour throughout the story. The writer's perspective in introducing the reverend brother's intellectual interpretation of authentic Biblical facts is so brilliant that it encourages you to fact check.

Ronald Clifford, Irish American Examiner. New York.

Cónal Creedon's new novel puts a magic-realist twist on the tale of a cleric's unrequited love for a nun. Brother Scully delves back through his analysis of scripture, which has led him to a unique and highly plausible theory regarding the true paternity of Jesus Christ. Inside the covers of *Begotten Not Made*, there unfolds a tale that's part poignant love story and part meditation on the phenomenon of faith, a uniquely Corkonian take on magical realism served up with Creedon's customary flair for colourful dialogue and tall tales – a fairy tale for the 21st Century.

 Ellie O'Byrne, ARTS, Irish Examiner.

Begotten Not Made is rewarding, straddling a fine line between pathos and comedy. We see the disintegration of Brother Scully – between the torment of his unrealised love and his unique take on Catholicism, he doesn't believe in the divinity of Jesus and has a theory as to his real paternity. This is a troubled man, literally crumbling into a despairing heap as an elderly man. Brother Scully elicits sympathy despite his obnoxiousness – a hard man to like but Creedon's talent is to draw out the humanity of this demented individual. There is a lot more to this novel than sexual and spiritual frustration – It is funny, and it has real charm. There are elements of magic realism here which give the novel an air of fairy-tale. *Begotten Not Made* is well written, strong on highly amusing dialogue and has a twist that is satisfying, well worth the wait. Like all good art, the local becomes universal with its truths and its understanding of human nature.

 Colette Sheridan, Weekend

Last night I finished Cónal Creedon's *Begotten Not Made*. It is multi-layered, funny and touching, at times madcap or magic realist, quintessential storytelling, and has a wonderful and satisfying ending. It's about the unrequited love between Brother Scully and Sister Claire, a novitiate in the convent across the valley from his monastery in Cork city. That spiritual affair began on the night in 1970 that Dana won the Eurovision Song Contest, and it lasts for almost fifty years – their correspondence continues: Scully and Claire send a signal to each other every morning at dawn by quickly switching their bedroom light off and on. That one single act of devotion gives Scully the courage to live out his chaste life. But not all is how it seems. And there is a sting in this tail.

 There are several poignant moments in the novel, the most moving of which is when towards the end of their hour or two together in 1970, in the garden, Scully and Claire are faced with a crucial decision. And that predicament, upon which their fates turned, reminded me of that great Cavafy poem, *Che fece... il gran rifiuto* (The Great Refusal)

Cónal has drawn a number of fine pen and ink illustrations to accompany the story which lends a charmingly quaint feeling to the rich reading experience.

Danny Morrison, Director of West Belfast Festival Féile an Phobail.

Begotten Not Made, a multi-faceted fairy-tale which gives a fresh twist to an ancient story – the life of Jesus. The book deftly presents an insight into human frailty: through the complicated love that arose between Br. Scully and Sr. Claire on the night Dana won the Eurovision. Equal parts hilarious and poignant. The story unfolds as Br. Scully grapples with his existence and his sanity and his unique exploration of the nature of belief. The book is also resplendent with illustrations by the author.

Aisling Meath, The Southern Star.

It's all there in *Begotten Not Made*, alongside the mysteries of the scripture, the alchemy of love, the pathos of life and the legend of a war hero racing pigeon: a picaresque epic that at times dips into the surreal.

Donal O'Donoghue, Books. RTÉ Guide.

Begotten Not Made is incredibly nuanced in that sympathy. Brother Scully is developed far beyond the definitions of his profession, beyond the collar, he is intellectual, emotional, sensitive and troubled. Such nuance is explored intricately in Cónal's classic, conversational style, ranging from profound humour to tinges of sadness and airs of dark comedy. The humour of the novel is colourful in every sense of the word, which Cónal infuses to dramatize the life of Brother Scully's adolescence. These playful anecdotes are threaded throughout the novel giving the lives of the characters depth and sincerity. At the end, the book is really set in that one hour, a feature reminiscent of Joyce.

Liz Hession, Motley Magazine.

What a rollicking good read it is. I have to confess that the Dowcha Boy pigeon business remained my favourite since it is so hilarious. But there were many such laugh out loud moments to be met with exclamation points in the margins. That whole Eurovision conceit was just brilliant. And coming round again and again to the flashing of the dawn lights. Loved the surreal moment when Scully walks off on the beam of light. And the great switcheroo of the ending was terrific. Wonderfully enjoyable book. Thanks a mill', Cónal!

David Monagan, Jaywalking With The Irish.

If there has been a sense that some documentaries on the Hidden Histories series have struggled to fully fill out the one-hour slot available, this was not the case with *Hidden History: The Burning of Cork* (RTÉ 1, Tuesday, 10:15pm). Instead, there was a sense that Neil Jordan (or indeed its own superb director, Cónal Creedon) could fruitfully be let loose on the story with a twenty-million-dollar budget. Creedon's documentary told far more than just the story of the night of December 11, 1920.

Village Magazine Dublin.

The Boys of Fairhill, Cónal Creedon's documentary which detailed the many accomplishments of 'the boys' in hurling, bowling, and dog-racing and pigeon fancying, indeed all the recreations which make a man's life worth living. The previous week Creedon had another erudite and evocative documentary about Cork, *If It's Spiced Beef*…and RTÉ is lucky to have him."

The Sunday Independent.

The impossibly surreal, hilarious, and often poignant series, *Under the Goldie Fish*
    Evening Herald.

For distinctive flavour, free rein to the imagination and even the odd passionate belief, there may never be a match for *Under the Goldie Fish*…Cónal Creedon's mad, bad, wonderful-to-know daily sitcom-soap… If you like your metafictions, intertextuality and just plain messin' in daily doses – Creedon's yer only man!"

The Irish Times.

Reviews of Readings by Cónal Creedon

Don't be fretting now about the past gone glories of Irish literary genius since we're lucky to have walking among us Cónal Creedon whom I not only had the personal pleasure of meeting as fellow author in the Sprachsalz festival [Austria] but heard the man read his work. The brilliance was self-evident and undeniable. The audience were in raptures over the beauty of his sentences and rapier-like wit. He writes about the human condition in ways that find you deep down where you just have to laugh and weep. Read this author and your faith will be restored in both literature and life.

Alan Kaufmann. – [Author of: Jew Boy, American Outlaw Book of Poetry]. Sprachsalz Festival Austria, 2016

The members of the Merriman Summer School were utterly enthralled by Cónal Creedon's presentation of a selection of his writings – a presentation that was warm, deeply insightful, and so humorous and entertaining about the human condition. He was by far one of the most able speakers at the school.

William J Smyth, Emeritus Professor UCC. Merriman Summer School, 2015

Cónal Creedon gave a tour de force reading of his work as it applies to the theme of 'love and marriage' at the 2015 Merriman Summer School in Ennis, Co. Clare. The audience reacted to Cónal's brilliant writing.

Professor Linda Connolly, Director Merriman Summer School, 2015

Cónal Creedon's presentation to Rochester in 2008 is still being spoken about. He established an easy and lasting rapport with the audience in his talk, Cork, the Center of the Universe as he shared slides that proved his point with humour and intelligence. It would be grand to have a return visit from this literary giant!

Elizabeth Osta – President of the Irish American Cultural Institute. (IACI) 7-city USA coast-to coast IACI Reading Tour

Cónal Creedon was a massive hit A festival highlight and I hope he will come back.

Pat McCabe – Flat Lake Festival, 2011

Cónal Creedon brought the house down at this year's Flat Lake Festival, any comic would envy the laughs he elicited from the audience.

Eoin Butler-Kennedy – The Irish Times – July 2011

A Humorous Reading Creedon reads from his work ... Creedon is a skilful reader, managing to keep the crowd engaged, a challenging feat for many writers who are often able to captivate with the written word and less with the spoken. Creedon is able to capture the simple moments of people's lives with honesty and humour.

The crowd finds his work quite humorous as he speaks of "battling the beast" (a pig) and anecdotes of St. Patrick, Protestantism, Catholicism, Freemasons, and other topics worthy of a laugh when written of skilfully. The passage relates the tale of the life, death, and funeral of the character's father. "It's a strange thing to carry your father in a box," he reads as detailing the humorous ordeal of trying to carry the father to the funeral in a coffin he himself handcrafted.

Shanghai International Literary Festival. Shanghai City Weekend – Trista Marie [Lit Review THAT'S Shanghai]

A mention, too, to Cónal Creedon. He is the A No. 1 writer of Cork, in my estimation, and absolutely should be known more broadly internationally; he has the ear for every corner conversation, every magnificent touch of endearing absurdity he encounters. He's known well enough in Ireland but should have longer stilts by far. Find him, try him. He went on for a half hour about his father's years' long construction of his own coffin and had every single mug laughing in stitches – about his father's intricately planned demise. Chalk this whole experience down to the category What I Love Best About Ireland. I mean – that you can dream about a man you never met

David Monaghan – Ireland Unhinged & Jaywalking With The Irish.

The Spring Literary festival [2010] was incredibly successful this year. Aside from the quality of the writers and some of the amazing performances (Cónal Creedon and Martin Espada especially wowed) audience figures were consistently large at each event. We were obliged to move to a bigger venue for the fourth day to avoid breaking fire regulations on overcrowding.

Pat Cotter – Artistic Director Munster Literature Centre, Éigse Literary festival 2010

Cónal Creedon at the Rock on The Fall's Road – stole the show and the hearts of everyone who heard him that afternoon. A highlight of the West Belfast Féile.
Danny Morrison, Director of West Belfast Festival Féile an Phobail

www.ingramcontent.com/pod-product-compliance
Lightning Source LLC
Chambersburg PA
CBHW021926040426
42448CB00008B/939